DIARY OF A
young soul rebel

BY ISAAC JULIEN AND COLIN MacCABE

WITH SCREENPLAY BY PAUL HALLAM AND DERRICK SALDAAN McCLINTOCK

BFI PUBLISHING

First published in 1991 by the
British Film Institute
21 Stephen Street, London W1P 1PL

Copyright © Isaac Julien and Colin MacCabe 1991

British Library cataloguing in Publication Data

Julien, Isaac
    Diary of a young soul rebel.
    I. Title II. MacCabe, Colin
    791. 430232

    ISBN 0851703100

Designed and typeset by Stella Crew, 2D Design Ltd.

Cover design by Giles Dunn for Neville Brody Studio

Printed in Great Britain by The Trinity Press, Worcester

Front cover photo by Sylvie Tata

Back cover photo by David A. Bailey

Photo credits text:
Sunil Gupta:
    pp. 29, 30, 32, 34/5, 36 (bottom), 38, 39, 40,41,
    44/45, 49, 52, 53, 55, 62, 63, 83, 84/5, 86/7, 88/9,
    90/1, 94 (bottom), 95 (bottom), 96/7, 98, 102, 118–24.
David A. Bailey:
    pp. 33, 36 (top), 57 (bottom), 60/1, 72, 76, 78/9, 80,
    82, 92, 94 (top), 95 (top), 99.

Contents

Acknowledgments

This book would not have been possible without the enthusiasm, support and skills of
Esther Johnson and Roma Gibson who were both amazing and a joy to work with.
Special thanks to Stella Crew of 2D Design for her immense patience and fun.

We would also like to thank Sunil Gupta and David A. Bailey for their brilliant photographs
and endless patience on the sets, Paul Hallam and Derrick Saldaan McClintock for their work on the script,
John Hewitt for his storyboard, and Mark Nash for his invaluable help with the manuscript.

For their generous support, both intellectually and emotionally, we are grateful to
Lina Gopaul, John Akomfrah, Karen Alexander, Paul Gilroy, Vron Ware, Stuart Hall, Bell Hooks, Steve Farrer,
Nadine Marsh-Edwards, Kobena Mercer, Tina Keane, Anna Thew, Sankofa and Black Audio Film Collective

Thanks to Henry Louis Gates Jnr, Anthony Appiah and Henry Finder for allowing us to include the interview
between Isaac Julien and Bell Hooks, which will appear in the fall '91 issue of *Transition* (no. 53 or NS 1,3).

The authors and publishers gratefully acknowledge permission to include in the film script quotes from
the following songs: 'Running Away' (Roy Ayers/Edwin Birdsong) and
'I'll Play the Fool' (August Darnell/Stony Browder Jr) – Warner Chappel Music Ltd.
'One Nation Under a Groove' (George Clinton/Garry M. Shider/Walter Morrison). © Copyright 1982 by
Bridgeport Music Inc., Southfield MI 48034. All rights reserved. Used by permission.

Isaac Julien

Introduction

The real starting point for *Young Soul Rebels* was the desire to make a film about 1977. That year was so important because on the one hand you had the incredible chauvinism of the Queen's Silver Jubilee and on the other there were very powerful counter narratives that outlined new kinds of national possibilities. Now everybody knows about the one called 'punk', which was at its height in 1977 and which was a very obvious opposition. But there was another counter narrative, much disdained by the left; which was the growth of a black popular culture particularly in terms of disco music – soul music. All the left had to say was that disco music was part of the capitalist music industry and that one should adopt the punk ethic of dismantling it. But what the left didn't realise was that their formulaic slogan 'black and white unite and fight' actually had some reality in this black popular culture.

At that time I felt very divided between politics and pleasure, between youth left organisations and the clubs. That division became a problem in terms of left discussions of the cinema, and more generally, in relation to life-style and politics. For me the mythic image of the soul boy and soul girl was extremely important as a way of discussing young black culture. But this culture was very marginalised politically and repressed historically. At the same time it meant that you were part of an elite group of style-makers. So to make a film about 1977 was to highlight all these conflicts, antagonisms, divisions, and to throw more light on black youth movements. One of the central points to be highlighted is how black culture remakes itself wherever it is placed. That's the condition of its survival – to continually reinvent itself as black culture. And 1977 was a very important moment of reinvention. Because there were no real examples of the signifying practices of black British culture in the dominant media, the youth movement had to do it by connection with the soul music from America often through the medium of Pirate Radio. Of course, with Soul II Soul, we take all that for granted now, but in 1977 it was hard to get hold of this black American music. It was diffi-cult to find icons, but the reinvention started around that music, opening up a space for a whole number of transgressions – both sexual and racial: these were the first clubs with black and white, straight and gay mixed in the audi-ences. That political and cultural excitement had never been figured in the dominant medias and I was determined to make people feel how exciting the moment was.

In this sense *Young Soul Rebels* is generational and reflects and speaks from the experiences of a generation – the experience of coming to terms with being black and British and asking yourself, 'Where is my place in British society?'. Reggae is part of the mythology of 1977 and there is no doubting its past and continuing importance, but reggae really relates back to the Caribbean whereas soul takes one into the wider black diaspora. Now, of course, everything is wonderfully hybrid. In 1977 a distinction between soul and reggae was more pronounced: one can almost make a set of political and cultural distinctions. Reggae was more tied up with black nationalism and certain rigidities of sex and race – tough masculine left politics. Soul, on the other hand, allowed for inter-racial relationships and challenged some of the structures of black masculinity. It opened up a less fixed and more fluid space and, of course, conventional left politics condemned this as anti-politi-cal, but that's where most of the energy for *Soul II Soul* or Kiss FM (the soul radio station) came from.

It is very important to stress the importance of this cultural resistance because that is where the younger generation of blacks are now finding hope and inspiration. The explicit discourse of say, the Anti-Nazi League, is just antiquarian now. What was important about the soul boys and girls was that they really overturned notions of British culture. It is from that space that you get the challenge to the hegemony of Englishness, the cry of 'I'm British, but...'. However, over and beyond that challenge, soul was the space in which the freaky–deeky and hybrid aspect of black cultural expression could really find an outlet. If you look at Britain now you can see a whole number of movements in art, film, photography and music where young blacks are engaged in debates, both with ourselves and with the dominant institutions. But this moment is also a moment of crisis because there is no political direction to these movements, and there are no significant black political leaders to appeal to.

But if you look at black music, particularly rap, then you find an area of political resistance which magazines like *Race Today* never managed to articulate. The problems with *Race Today* and the reasons for its eventual collapse, is that it had a far too conventional leftist discourse to cope with the cultural reality of Britain. The result was that people like me, who started off looking for political direction, soon found it very inadequate. Most of the classical discourse of the left was simply hopeless in the face of what was happening.

Ironically, the fascist right seemed to get the cultural and political point much quicker. In 1979 the youth magazine of the National Front, *Bulldog*, could write: 'The record and the cassette is more powerful than television or the newspapers where youth is concerned. Disco and its melting pot pseudo-philosophy must be fought or Britain's streets will be full of black worshipping soul boys. ' And that's just a more articulate version of Thatcher's 'swamping' speech or Powell's English nationalism.

It's impossible even to get interested in the debate on black sections when nothing of the reality of Britain seems to get through to the Labour Party. They really cannot address the crucial questions of national identity which were so clearly posed over a decade ago with the Jubilee. The experience for a black person of being silenced and excluded was, and is, very unpleasant. It's this nasty British habit of waving the flag which, with all its connotations of Empire and colonialism, inevitably excludes black people and forces us to question the construction of national identities. Paul Gilroy has dealt with this magnificently in *There Ain't no Black in the Union Jack* (Hutchinson, 1987) as have Stuart Hall and Homi Bhabha. I have tried to capture this in fiction. It seems a particularly appropriate moment as we go into 1992 because in the celebration of the new Europe we had better find cultural spaces for the Afro-Germans, the black Parisians, and for us, the black British.

The Genesis of the Film

Nadine Marsh-Edwards, 1991
Photo by Charlie Best

Nadine Marsh-Edwards (Producer of the film) and I had always wanted to make a film both about being young and addressed to a youth audience. More basically, we wanted to make a film about our experiences of growing up. And in a way, much of the work from Sankofa* – *Passion of Remembrance* (Maureen Blackwood and Isaac Julien, 1986), *Dreaming Rivers* (Martine Attille, 1987) and *Perfect Image* (Maureen Blackwood, 1988) – related to that desire. But after *Passion of Remembrance* we wanted to make a film which would be more narrative, and both Nadine and Derrick Saldaan McClintock wanted to make a film that would deal with a number of questions around masculinity and sexual and racial identity.

The first treatments and drafts were just attempts to find a story which would highlight being seventeen in London in 1977 and which would turn around this sub-culture that was as exciting as punk and which people still didn't know much about.

We also knew from the start that this was a film that we wanted to develop with the British Film Institute. Almost all our work until then had been done with Channel 4 (with Alan Fountain and Rod Stoneman). They had been incredibly supportive but they worked with intentions that never quite matched their institutional will. The budgets they allocated for black films were limited and to develop fiction films with budgets over £400,000 was almost impossible for them. There was no doubt in our minds that what they really wanted from black film-makers were documentaries of a realist nature,

---

*Sankofa Film and Video is a pioneering group of young black film-makers who have produced radical drama for cinema and television over the past eight years.

although Sankofa and Black Audio Film Collective were allowed to make experimental films under their remit of innovation.

There were various reasons why we approached the British Film Institute. We thought that they would offer us more scope and give us a chance to make a film that was addressed to cinema audiences. Colin MacCabe had visited us soon after his appointment as Head of Production and made clear that he was open to a wide variety of projects, and Jim Pines, who was the BFI's Ethnic Minority Advisor at the time, encouraged us to make an application. Generally we felt we had a good chance of getting help with developing a script and going through a number of drafts.

This impression was reinforced by our first meetings with Colin, who impressed us with his enthusiasm for the project. At the same time we began to realise how difficult it was to write this kind of mainstream script. Initially the realism of the text was broken up by the use of a duppy, a kind of Caribbean ghost, who commented on the story. Then Derrick Saldaan McClintock (co-writer of the script for *Young Soul Rebels*) and I went to see *Sammy and Rosie Get Laid* (Stephen Frears, 1987) and we were totally freaked out by its use of a ghost, and even more by the fact that we didn't think that the ghost worked.

The next step came at a meeting with Colin regarding the first draft of the script. He said that although the material was interesting there was not enough story and he suggested that there must be something from our own experience which would provide us with a narrative. Derrick started talking about his experience of being arrested on suspicion of an East End murder and Colin said that sounded very promising. So we started working on that and the more we worked on it the more excited we became because it really did develop a kind of narrative drive. But as we developed the narrative we also found that the whole process became more and more difficult technically as the plot became more complex.

It was at this point that we got Paul Hallam in on the script as an experienced writer and he made the murder aspect of the film more serious. He wanted to draw out the consequences of the murder, the way it meant different things to different groups. What does the murder of a gay black man mean to the police, to the black community, and to gay people generally? This development also enabled us to talk about different types of black masculinity. In this way the film dramatises a whole series of debates through the reactions to the murder.

Homosexuality and Hybridity

In 1977 the consumer development which currently produces endlessly demarcated spaces – black clubs, gay clubs, etc. – wasn't so well established. The great thing about clubs like *Lacy Lady* (a soul club in Seven Kings, Ilford) or *Global Village* (another soul club in Charing Cross, where *Heaven*, a gay disco, is now) was their wonderfully hybrid space – black/white, gay/straight. This space opened up a whole variety of simultaneous transactions – the excitement and importance of which one could see on the dance floor but nobody was writing about or recording. For me these clubs really offered a range of experience that gay clubs could not. The gay clubs were important but they were a very white space; there was a sense in which you had to leave parts of yourself outside the door. At one and the same time they excluded part of you and fetishised an-'Other'. In the same way, the magazines of the period which dealt with gay issues like *Gay Left* and *The Leveller*, important as they were, were so concerned with 'coming out' that they weren't really interested in the specific complexities of being black and gay. But what they articulated politically meant that my generation has been able to take a number of questions around sexual identity for granted.

For me, clubs like *Global Village* offered a much more utopian space than the gay scene and it is that utopianism which is present in the film and in the friendship between Chris and Caz. Chris just accepts Caz's sexuality without really thinking very much about it in terms of race and sex. In a sense the film is about a bringing to consciousness of the possibilities of those clubs. And it is those possibilities which mark the most exciting moments in contemporary popular culture, although there is also a reactive pressure against those moments in the development of a new pseudo 'Nation of Islam' and a kind of black politics which is interested in re-articulating homophobia. The film really celebrates the black cultural contribution to youth culture and it is that contribution which still is one of the most optimistic developments today.

This text was produced from a long interview between Isaac Julien and Colin MacCabe in January 1991. Colin MacCabe then edited the resulting text and it was finally revised by Isaac Julien.

Introduction

BFI Production

The British Film Institute Production Board has its origin in the Experimental Film Fund set up by Michael Balcon in 1953. The aim of this fund, which came from the industry, was to allow people within the industry to make their first short films. Administered by the British Film Institute it had an autonomous existence and selection was by a board chosen from within the industry. In the first decade of its existence it was remarkably successful – among those who made their first films with it were Lindsay Anderson, Karel Reisz, and Alain Tanner. In the mid-sixties the new Labour government, with Jennie Lee as Minister of Arts, made the decision to supplement the fund, now almost exhausted, with Eady Levy money and to integrate it into the British Film Institute. At the beginning of the seventies there was an attempt to give the British Film Institute Production Board, as it was now called, a much bigger role. In addition to the short films it had always produced (Stephen Frears' first film was shot in 1969), it would attempt to break into the feature market. This attempt failed for a variety of reasons, most significantly, lack of money.

In 1974 Peter Sainsbury took over as Head of Production and the Board took a really new direction. A full history of that period would fill a book by itself but for our purposes we can isolate two significant developments. First, the original purpose of the fund, which was to finance first short films for people within the industry, assumed a thriving industry. This assumption no longer applied by the mid-sixties and, indeed, the failed attempt to move into feature production was one response to this crisis. By 1974, however, there were a new set of potential film-makers being produced by the tertiary education system who had, in any case, little desire to work in the mainstream industry. The dominant aesthetic was post-68 and anti-representational. Narrative and spectacle were to be eschewed in favour of analysis and political correctness. The majority of films made during this period were as dire as such an aesthetic suggests (although great talents such as Bill Douglas were also funded), but the over-theoreticism did allow a genuine concentration on the problems of independent production. Thus, when the decision was made in 1979 to move back into features with Chris Petit's *Radio On*, there was an understanding that it was not enough simply to fund films but that the Board should provide help at other levels. Over the next five years the Production Division grew as it acquired not only production expertise but took on the tasks of domestic distribution and international sales. The argument for these developments was that a subsidy system which simply funded films was ignoring the reality of the cinema as a system of production and distribution. Even the most talented director needed to draw on production expertise which would not be available at the low budget levels where the British Film Institute operated. Furthermore, a film was not finished until it was seen and, once again, the low level of returns would not place BFI films high up any distribution company or sales agent's agenda.

All these developments, including the early aesthetic, bore magnificent fruit with Peter Greenaway's *The Draughtsman's Contract* (1982). In the funding of the film however, one very important new element was now in play: Channel 4. And Channel 4 affected every level of British film-making below the mega-budgets of Goldcrest *et al.* In the early eighties it was the Channel which allowed the British Film Institute to undertake many more feature films as it provided additional resources by acquiring much of the Institute's back catalogue. However, in 1985, the whole future of BFI Production was thrown into doubt by the Conservative government's Films Bill, which coincided with Peter Sainsbury's departure to work as an independent producer.

The Films Bill abolished the Eady level, the major source of BFI production money. Without any substantive funds to distribute, the overhead entailed in running a small studio (some ten full-time employees) became difficult to justify and there was a considerable body of opinion among the governors of the Institute that Production should revert to being a simple dispenser of subsidy along a more traditional model.

It was in this context that I was appointed Head of Production. As someone who had long admired Peter Sainsbury, I was determined to build on his foundations. I was very aware that the current crisis – no money and the threat of closure – obscured the fact that there was a very impressive past record and enormous potential for the future. All this, however, depended on future funding. Anthony Smith, the then director of the Institute, came up with a scheme by which he persuaded Jeremy Isaacs, a past Chairman of the Board, to promise half a million pounds a year from Channel 4 if the government would match that money. Until then Channel 4 had been buying films individually; now they would acquire the Television licence on any films that we produced. The deal was typical of Channel 4's shrewd generosity. If the government were persuaded to increase its grant (which it did) then the money was well spent. If I was able to use the resulting £1,000,000 as a basis to raise more money, then the Channel would do very well.

With the financial future secured, I was able to concentrate on building on Sainsbury's foundation in the division. If we had all the elements to function as a tiny studio on the margins, I wanted to make sure that we did it as professionally on a shoe-string as the boys in the Armani jackets and stretch limos. Also, in order to complete our full range of activities as a studio, we needed to have a proper development strategy, and, indeed, it was in the development of new writers and new kinds of scripts that I saw my primary task. In this I was enormously aided by the Board and particularly by its chair, Margaret Matheson. My very general aesthetic was a desire to provide a record of experiences which even in this too much recorded age had been dismissed as unworthy; to bear witness to lives whose stories had not yet been thought worthy of inclusion within more general histories. It is this which I hope unites the very diverse films made during my time as Head of Production, even those which had been developed before I took up my post. From the homoerotics of art in *Caravaggio* (Derek Jarman, 1986) to the farmers and fishermen of *On the Black Hill* (Andrew Grieve, 1987) and *Venus Peter* (Ian Sellar, 1989), from the pre-consumerist Liverpudlian working class of *Distant Voices Still Lives* (Terence Davies, 1988) to the post modern urban youth of *The Love Child* (Robert Smith, 1987), from the political experience of *Friendship's Death* (Peter Wollen, 1987) and *Melancholia* (Andi Engel, 1989) to the ethics and technology of vision in *Degrees of Blindness* (Cerith Wyn Evans, 1988), the aim was to find fresh images and new sounds for the British screen.

Besides this very general aim, however, there was a very conscious decision to attempt to develop ways of recording the new generations born to Commonwealth immigrants. *Young Soul Rebels* was a direct result of this policy and the first script of this type to be produced as a feature by the Institute, although this general emphasis had already resulted in an extraordinarily brilliant short film: Gurinder Chadha's *I'm British But...* (1989). In giving the institutional background to *Young Soul Rebels*, it is also worth pointing out that in its funding the film is a European production with money from Kinowelt in Germany, La Sept in France and Iberoamericana in Spain. If the film is difficult to imagine without an institution such as BFI Production, it is yet another example of the influence of Channel 4 who, in addition to their subvention to the BFI, provided directly half of the 1. 2 million pound budget. In this context it is important to acknowledge the crucially supportive role of Colin Leventhal, Head of Acquisition and Sales at Channel 4 and the one ubiquitous presence in all the various deals between Channel 4 and the BFI.

Diary of a Young Soul Rebel

If the film was years in the making and planning, this book was a more spontaneous generation. As I explain in my diary, I gave up the post of Head of Production in the summer of 1989 and became the Head of Research and Information. Although I was to continue to act as an executive producer on *Young Soul Rebels*, my major concerns in the Institute were no longer just production, where Ben Gibson succeeded me, but took in a range of tasks including publishing.

It was at a publishing planning meeting just before shooting started that I had the idea of a diary. At one level it is simply an attempt to feed what is an ever-growing market. The success of Stephen Bach's *Final Cut: Dreams and Disaster in the Making of 'Heaven's Gate'* (Cape, 1985) or Jake Ebert and Terry Ilotts's book on Goldcrest, *My Indecision is Final*, (Faber, 1990) testify to an increasing appetite for behind the scenes tales of film-making as well as film scripts. This book contributes to that genre and I trust is of sufficient interest at that general level.

There was, however, a slightly more sophisticated ambition in setting Isaac and myself this task. If there have been many film-makers who have come from the theatre and many who have come from criticism, it is a relatively new phenomenon to find people working in production who have participated in the recent growth of film theory. I hoped that the diaries might reflect on this new formation.

In choosing this form there are many limitations. The view produced is inevitably partial; over 100 people worked on the film and all would have different diaries, stressing different contributions. There is also a rather arbitrary start date (the diary could in fact have gone back over five years). But the aim is not to provide something complete and comprehensive but rather to give a flavour of the quotidian reality of production, how creative decisions get made in an atmosphere where time and technique are money, where personality is crucial and where variables, such as the weather, suddenly affect the possibilities of a shot or a scene.

It is an inevitability that such a form generates quite a lot of heat as well as light. It is perhaps worth pointing out that all the conflicts and doubts that arose during the production did have happy endings. There is no doubt that all the cast and crew of the film performed magnificently and, if there were conflicts, that is part and parcel of even the most equable and easy production.

Finally, if it is clear what the director does, what on earth is an executive producer? It must be said that this credit covers a multitude of sins, from indicating the guy who signed the cheques, to the person who raised the money, to the individual who initiated the project, to the one who takes institutional responsibility for it. If the early development and major financing of *Young Soul Rebels* were my responsibility, the final revisions of the script and the completion of the financial circle were largely overseen by Ben Gibson. Nadine Marsh-Edwards, not only bore the detailed responsibility for the production of the film but had also been involved with the initial conception of the project.

But the film for me is much more than an individual credit. It marks, together with *Hallelujah Anyhow* (Matthew Jacobs, 1991), the completion of an ambition that I had set for myself and BFI Production in 1985. That aim was to celebrate the possibilities of the polyglot and miscegenated society that Britain now is. There is no wish to hide or play down the daily brutalities of racism but a deep desire to alert people to the utopian possibilities opened up by the breaking of the national mould and its sexual and cultural consequences. It is that desire which animates the range of my work, from the literary criticism on Joyce and Milton to the bureaucratic involvement in setting up European distribution systems. It would be all too easy to characterise *Young Soul Rebels* as a black movie or a gay movie, and it is, of course both of those but, for me, it is a European hybrid, the very form of our future.

It is also, and most importantly, a movie. I am one of that generation who, seduced by the Leninist programme of the reduction to the political, had contributed to the dismal aesthetic which informed so much of the Production Board work in the mid-seventies. But, in a further generational development, I am also part of a reaction which, while refusing to drop political concerns and projects, was determined to respect the autonomy of other levels of experience, particularly art. The problems and contradictions of the Leninist position are most painfully evident in Bertolt Brecht's short 'Organum for the Theatre' (in *Brecht on Theatre*, ed. and trans. John Willett, Methuen, 1964). This brilliant text, with its explicit reference back to Bacon and Aristotle, attempts to resituate art in relation to what is seen as the scientific advance provided by historical materialism. But Brecht, throughout the text, is caught between two arguments. On the one hand, and this is the dominant discourse, he wants to argue that all art can do is to present the truths discovered by the science of history to the agents of that history. The problem with such a position is that, in the final analysis, it deprives art of any function except that of transmission of truths articulated elsewhere. It falls into exactly the problems of neo classical theories attempting to situate art in relation to the monumental advances of Newtonian science. It is Alexander

Pope's magnificently despairing

> True wit is nature to Advantage Dress'd
> What oft was thought but ne'er so well expressed
> *An Essay in Criticism*, 1711

where art (wit) becomes limited to mere questions of expression, the basic thought is elsewhere; for Pope Newtonian nature, for Brecht Marxist history. There is a second and more subterranean discourse in 'A Short Organum', however, in which Brecht argues a much more radical position in which art is actually the space of certain kinds of epistemic discovery, where art produces new forms of knowledge, knowledge which is intimately related to pleasure. This second discourse, which imposes itself on anyone who wishes to argue both for the historicity and the reality of a particular art form, sits very uneasily with traditional Marxism. Its proper elaboration would necessitate, in accordance with Brecht's own project, a real evaluation of art in relation to other forms of knowledge. This is why philosophy of science remains the key discipline for the new forms of cultural studies which are now appearing.

Without presuming upon that elaboration, what has been said makes clear that the political content of film (or any other work of art) is not necessarily given in advance. If it is, the film is likely to remain trapped very precisely in its own time, unable to do more than mouth already existing ideas. To give voice to new possibilities the film must make new realities and new pleasures available. Whether *Young Soul Rebels* does this cannot be certain in advance. I hope that it opens out the Utopian possibilities that I see and hear on the streets of London. For that to be true then the soul clubs of 1977 must have been as crucial a space as Isaac Julien describes in his introduction, and the film-maker and all the cast and crew must have realised that space for others. The aim of this book is to bear witness to some of the elements that went into that realisation, to testify to the effort to transform that space into time.

TABLE A

THE RT HON THE PRIME MINISTER
The Lord Brabourne
Sir David Berriman
The Rt Hon The Lord Barnett
Sir Richard Attenborough
Mr Simon Relph
Mr David Plowright
Mr Lew Wasserman

TABLE B

THE RT HON NICHOLAS RIDLEY
Sir Ian Trethowan
Mr John Woodward
Mrs Carolyn Lambert
Professor Colin Young
Mr John Boorman
Mr Jeremy Thomas
Mr Otto Plaschkes

LUNCHEON

10 DOWNING STREET
FRIDAY, 15TH JUNE 1990

Mr Isaac Julien

TABLE C

THE RT HON RICHARD LUCE
Mr David Puttnam
Mr Percy Livingstone
Mr Michael Williams-Jones
Mr Alan Sapper
Ms Ann Skinner
Mr Charles Wesoky
Mr Mamoun Hassan

TABLE D

MR ERIC FORTH
Mr Wilf Stevenson
Miss Susan Brown
Mr Edward Lee
Mr Jake Eberts
Mr Barry Potter
Mr James Daly
Mr Simon Linnett

TABLE E

MR PETER SMITH
Mr Bob Phillis
Mr Larry Chrisfield
Mr Simon Perry
Mr David Scott
Ms Premila Hoon
Mr Nik Powell

TABLE F

PROFESSOR BRIAN GRIFFITHS
Ms Lynda Myles
Mr Isaac Julien
Mr Barry Jenkins
Mr David Rose
Mr Nigel Stafford-Clarke
Ms Sarah Radclyffe
Mr Stephen Moore

Diaries

● Isaac Julien
Downing Street Seminar Saturday 16 June

I woke up very early this morning at 7 o'clock, got into the bath and of course Rosemarie (my Personal Assistant) rang the bell. She was dead on time as usual; very boring – Rosemarie's always dead on time. Well, she has to be, working with someone like me. I didn't really have time to arrange my folders or do the necessary things that one would do if one was going to a meeting in 10 Downing Street but I thought, why should I really bother about being precise when I've got so many things on? I mean, I haven't got time to go to 10 Downing Street anyway. Rosemarie seemed to be in a very bad mood; she drove me through the West End and just seemed to be taking all the wrong turnings. Why can't she just drive there like most people would drive? [laugh] When we got to Whitehall she drove like a stranger in a new town. Anyway, before going to the meeting, I had a toasted cheese sandwich in an Italian bar in Westminster. Then, of course, we were late. I was supposed to get there at a quarter past nine, the seminar starts at half past, you can't be late. We got there at twenty past. We drove up to the gate which blocks access to Downing Street and a policeman said, 'You can't go any further.' [I think Rosemarie had decided that she was going to drive me right into Downing Street.] She was into it much more than I was. I got out of the car, walked up Downing Street and of course all the Press were there. A door was open at the end of Downing Street where I thought everybody was going. I nearly walked into it until a policeman stopped me, saying, 'Where are you going?' So I said, 'I'm going to the conference', and he said, 'Well, you have to go into 10 Downing Street.' I turned around and everybody was laughing – all the media people. [I thought to myself, well just trust me to do something like that.] I walked in. Actually, when you get inside Number 10 it really expands – it's huge, masses of rooms, velvety carpet, lots of paintings and flower arrangements. It was ordered, tidy, servants milling around from room to room, people watching you. There seemed to be hundreds of people. Then I was told to go upstairs. Photographic prints and patriotic paintings covered the whole side of the wall as you walk up. Went into the reception room and quite a few people were already there. Everyone who was at the meeting the previous day was there, but more dressed up: Jeremy Thomas (Executive Producer of *The Last Emperor*), David Puttnam (Britain's most famous Producer), Lynda Myles (Commissioning Editor for Independents at the BBC), Wilf Stevenson (Director of the British Film Institute), Richard Attenborough, Sarah Radclyffe (Producer for Working Title), Simon Relph ([then] Chief Executive of British Screen). There wasn't anybody from Channel 4; there were no television people really. The head ACTT guy, Alan Sapper, was there (behaving in the typical masculinist, cliche style of a trades union spokesman). There was an Asian woman, Premila Hoon, who works for Guinness-Mahon Film Financiers. Nobody seemed to know what to do; everybody seemed to be slightly disjointed. Most people were standing up, but I thought, I'm just going to sit down. A few people said hello, but not many; everyone was slightly nervous. And then the Prime Minister walked in and for that split second it was like seeing a Spitting Image puppet; it was just weird, and she looked vacant and tired. However, she was polite, showed everybody into another room and we all sat down. It was really a very private affair.

When I first sat down I was in-between Linda Myles and Jeremy Thomas, then everybody got up and went to the front row because it was empty. Jeremy Thomas then came back to my row, but a sat a seat away from me; like on the tube – white people don't want to be close, it's funny.

Richard Attenborough spoke first. You realise how skilful he is in talking to people, making them feel comfortable; he's a great actor and is able to use all his resources to make sure the show runs smoothly. He gave a kind of outline introduction to the Prime Minister which was very jovial and chatty but informational. Everyone then gave a precis of their papers. It was a bit like going back to school; everyone had done their homework. Schoolmarm Maggie sitting down and all the boys and girls being good students. In fact, the whole thing is like that: everyone gets up, makes their little introduction and speaks very politely. Highly pretentious really – a bit like being in Parliament!

Margaret Thatcher conducted the whole affair with absolute control. She pretends to be charming, and seductive, and on observation, I could see that she uses her gender in terms of being feminine, listening to men, in the way she'd ask questions, and then she'll be like a mother and tell the men off.

When we broke for coffee, it was like being in another meeting: people came up and asked you questions. Otto Plashkes from The Producers Association was a real pain – he seemed unbearably arrogant. What struck me was that the women, including Margaret Thatcher, acknowledged me and were fairly friendly but most of the men made me feel invisible, which was to be expected. It was heavy-going but Richard Attenborough (Dickie) tried his best to make one feel comfortable.

During the break, just before we were going back for the second sitting, Ann Scott (a well-known producer) had some biscuits and she put them down. Margaret Thatcher said, 'Take them with you, come on! I have to worry about my figure, I can't eat too many; you should eat them, bring them in with you!' [as if it were some lower-middle class home!] She said a few strange things about arts subsidies. I mean, obviously she was very careful not to antagonise the film industry verbally and she seemed in some sense to be in awe of it, but at the same time she realised that we weren't able to compete in Europe because of the immense subsidy systems that exist there with Government support. Amending ties with Europe seemed to be the main theme behind her suggestions and she knew that her track record hadn't been good with the British film industry so she was going to make up with both the constituencies by investing £5 million into British Screen which would go towards European co-productions (although £5 million won't go anywhere, will it?). Two working parties were going to be set up to allow for some kind of debate and policy directives with the Department of Trade and Industry.

In relation to talking about subsidies and film finance for independents, there was just a big, big question mark. The film industry was being discussed in a very mainstream way; the 'Independent sector' had no voice really except through Wilf Stevenson and myself I suppose. I wasn't totally convinced I should have been there at all.

I must admit that David Puttnam looked thoroughly miserable; I don't think he really enjoyed being there. Jeremy Thomas looked quite fed up too. Margaret Thatcher and Nicholas Ridley kept looking at me all the time. So did another guy - one of Mrs Thatcher's confidants. I felt like an impostor being there... The other surprising thing was that after the seminar I realised there were a few black people in Number 10. Mostly in servant positions, of course, but there was a younger black women who looked like she did something important, so that was kind of encouraging. I caught the eye of another black waiter. It was strange because I thought there wouldn't be any other black people there. I could only think of Number 10 as the 'Institution of Whiteness' basically, and you wouldn't think black people would be let in the front door. But they let me in. How strange...

Simon Perry made a rather convoluted argument about making a film for America with all American money, and saying that he had no British money. Sarah Radclyffe spoke about co-production for Europe and how difficult it is for British producers now. John Woodward, the new Chief Executive of The Producers Association, made this ridiculous speech about tax incentives for American stars to enable them to come to Britain and not be taxed, which I thought was a boring right-wing argument.

Most of the arguments made throughout the Seminar were interesting because they revolved around Europe. Although we are potentially in a very central position to European film production and can be exploited, we can't match our monies with our competitors' because the continental European producers can lay more cash on the table. It's a non competitive start for British producers. But at the same time we are the envy of Europe because we've got the English language. David Puttnam gave a big speech for the National Film School about training. He used the example of Michael Caton-Jones who directed *Scandal* (1989), saying that if people invest in training, young directors like Caton-Jones make money for Britain – it was a good economic argument which was very progressive compared with what some of the other people were saying.

Margaret Thatcher was very much into appeasing everybody. You realise that if you got on the wrong side of her, that mother bit would really come out. She treated the men like boys and they loved it. It was weird. It's ironic being in a space like that, to think that the Government has totally run down the country and destroyed so many things. There is something quite hypocritical about partaking in an event like this, but of course I was totally fascinated to see and experience Number 10. An 'agenda for change' was agreed, including action to stimulate European co-production; support for marketing initiatives; and commitment to investigate fiscal and structural reforms (see *The View from Downing Street* by Jane Headland and Simon Relph, BFI Publishing, 1991).

I wanted to speak about how the possibility of getting funding for a film like *Young Soul Rebels* is made totally impossible because of the Government's attitude to European initiatives such as the Media Programme and Eurimages. In the course of Wilf Stevenson's talk, he said that I was to begin shooting in a fortnight and shouldn't really be here, to which the Prime Minister said, 'Oh, really?... And can we have the next person?' I suppose I should have made an intervention there and then but I thought to myself, why should I? But I felt a bit set up – the token black. I had something prepared, but I decided not to fulfil their expectations. I think people were suspicious of this. I'm sure Richard Attenborough felt that I should have said something and Wilf Stevenson asked why I hadn't made an intervention. Although I did manage to say a few things afterwards, I didn't really see the point when so many things were sewn up and premeditated.

There was an agenda, the outcome of various drafts, outlining the structure of the debate. It was funny at the beginning when Margaret Thatcher said, 'Come on, let's have a debate; come on, I really want to hear you.' She's really into it [laugh] and you see Nicholas Ridley turning around and looking at her thinking, 'Oh my God!'

I suppose I should conclude by saying that I didn't really want to commit myself to the whole scenario and so, for me, keeping silent was a weapon against not exposing myself.

When the seminar finished we were joined by other people from the industry – like David Rose (the original Commissioning Editor for Drama for Channel 4) and Colin Young (Director of the National Film School) – who came for lunch. It almost felt like another meeting. I went to the toilet. Simon Relph came too and seemed quite pleased with how everything went [laugh]. He'd read the script of *Young Soul Rebels* and had said that it carried two crosses: the gay cross and the black one (not very supportive, but still). I think he thinks I'm a bit of a rebel, so it doesn't really matter, does it? I'm making the film now anyway at the budget we wanted (£1. 2 million). Being in the toilet was one of the most amusing parts of being in Number 10 because it was so shabby. It was on the way that I noticed some more black people; I really looked and thought, oh, there are black people in Number 10 (all three of them).

Having the lunch was fairly boring. The tables were all arranged alphabetically: on my table there was Lynda Myles, Sarah Radclyffe, David Rose, this guy from Cannon and then this other guy (I didn't know who he was) and then the confidant of Margaret Thatcher. It looked like the rebels' table and was certainly a more interesting table than other ones, that's for sure. But I had to sit next to this boring Cannon guy who was going on and on about cinema audience figures rising as a result of their British multiplexes and their improved screening facilities, etc. etc. David Rose began having an argument with him saying they don't show enough British films in Cannon cinemas, that they are all American. The Cannon guy retorted that if British films were good enough, people would go to see them. Rose said this was total rubbish because the publicity budgets for all those Hollywood films matched the total budget of many British films and even if the American Hollywood film isn't that good you still have to see it in England because we've become a dumping ground. As long as Cannon people get their salary cheques, that's all that seems to be really important; nothing else matters.

When I first told my mother about going to see the Prime Minister, she asked if I could give her a good two or three kicks for her. When I spoke to her afterwards she asked if I had [laugh]. I said no, and she was most upset.

The press conference was fine but Derek Malcolm blanked me. Basically, the press were saying, 'Five million isn't much money; don't you think you should have asked for more?'

After the event it was like being in shock. I'd been to 10 Downing Street! [laugh] I had to go straight to Aldwych station to sort out the possibility of using it as a location for the film. We had a *Young Soul Rebels* mini get-together at a tapas bar and then I went to dinner with Colin and Flavia. People thought it went OK. It was bizarre, because you could see how antagonistic Margaret Thatcher can be (we've all seen it on television!), but she acted quite politely. She said weird things like, 'The subsidies are far too high in Europe; it's really unfair that we are competing. We must try to get them down.' I kept thinking that was such a mad philosophy, to think that Germany or France would put subsidies down because Margaret Thatcher thinks they are too high.

Part of me just hated going to 10 Downing Street today. I hated the fiasco. I had to go to Paul Smith to buy a suit and stuff like that – you know... black people don't go to Downing Street every day. If you go there, you've got to look how your mother and father would like you to look [laugh]. It's all a big image game really.

◆ Colin MacCabe
Friday 15 June

I started the day with a terrible interview on Radio 4. All the grown-ups are going off to see Ma Thatcher – I am dispatched to the *Today* programme where John Humphries demands to know why on earth the film industry needs subsidy when successful films make money. I trot out all the arguments about the impossibility of recovering your money in your own territory, and that therefore there is a need for subsidy if you want films about the reality of Britain. But I sound desperately unconvincing – even to myself. I only warm to my theme when I get in a plug for *Young Soul Rebels*. Without subsidy, I say, we would never be making a film by a young black film-maker.

The problem is that I don't, as such, believe in the need for subsidy at all. The Downing Street delegation is in fact representing bad economic and cultural arguments. The bad economics is that there should be subsidy to allow us to compete with Hollywood. Which is also the cultural mistake. It's not that Hollywood films are necessarily bad – many, if not most, are incredibly good but they are produced out of a massive industry which demands very specific skills to address its mass audience. Its scriptwriters, actors and technicians are brilliant at producing movies within the available formulas. We just don't have enough people working in this way to match those particular talents. You can't be a smaller version of Hollywood for both economic and cultural reasons.

What we are good at is making smaller, local films where the intense desire to represent experience not available in the Hollywood movies is what is of value both in aesthetic and economic terms. The problem is that when production companies have successes at this level they are soon driven by the ineluctable logic of development and overhead costs into trying to succeed in the bigger American market where almost all fail unless like Puttnam, Attenborough or Thomas they become stars in their own right. Not to mention the fact that while Hollywood will rely on its own training grounds for much of the creative and technical side, it is always on the look-out for talented directors it can employ in its factory. So the poor little British production company sees one of its own major assets disappear onto Concorde in a haze of cigar smoke to the background music of very large cheques being signed. In fact, I make a joke about this on the radio programme when I say that in five years' time Isaac won't even bid me the time of day. I'm only half-joking – I can see Isaac in the Marquis on Sunset without any difficulty at all.

The subsidy we need is the subsidy we've got. What nobody mentions when they moan about the ridiculously small subsidies for British films is that for the last ten years Channel 4 has put over £10,000,000 a year into films. Commercial television has subsidised the British art cinema of the 1980s but this subsidy is effectively at the whim of the Channel's Chief Executive. Jeremy Isaacs decided that he would use the Channel to revive the British cinema and he did. A successor could as easily decide that he wants his drama straight on the screen without bothering with the pitfalls and pleasures of cinema. As importantly, the cost of cinema has risen much faster than inflation and the Channel no longer gets as big a bang for its buck.

What is desperately needed is to draw on the lessons of the past ten years and come up with a plan for European cinema. This is ostensibly what the Downing Street Seminar is about. But Thatcher's ignorance about economics and our own industry's fixation on the States means that the enormous chances offered by Europe in the 90s are bound to be missed.

What really needs to be said to Thatcher is that she has invented through Channel 4 a perfect model of subsidy to offer to Europe. The problem with massive subsidies in Europe are that they are often, as in Germany, completely unrelated to any audience either in the cinema or in television. The result is that huge numbers of low-budget German films are made but nobody ever sees them. The politics of the selection committee determine what gets chosen and nobody cares whether the film gets seen or not. In Britain in the 1980s most funding decisions have been the responsibility of individuals who therefore have a very personal stake in a film's success. Also almost all funds have been influenced by Channel 4 who have (perhaps their most important cultural contribution) insisted on driving very hard commercial deals and on attracting as much commercial money into a production as possible. This mix of subsidy and market is crucial. If there is no attention to the market there is also no attention to an audience. But you may need to add subsidy to a given market if it is going to produce the goods you want. It is at this point that I feel very distant from those gathered in Downing Street. Because the questions – what goods do you want produced? what films do you want made? – are the ones that will be ducked. We will pretend that with a little bit of help we can compete with Hollywood while the reality is that we will certainly fail at that. A little bit of help now would produce a vital European film industry but I'm not certain how many people in Downing Street either want that or understand the kind of cultural and economic argument which underpins it. Much of my last five years has been occupied with trying to find ways forward for European film but between the Brussels bureaucracy and Thatcherite thuggery one can get a little dispirited.

The news from Downing Street is that there will be £5,000,000 for Europe spread over three years. As an absolute sum it is ludicrously little – but if the terms of the fund were right it could get many more British producers into Europe. It will be interesting to see how it develops over the summer.

At the end of the day I go for a drink with the crew in a Tapas bar on the Pentonville Road. It says something about my middle-aged life that this is the first I've been in. The place is full to overflowing with young, very drunk people. I'm both embarrassed and flattered to be swarmed over by one of the young girls at the bar. Her behaviour becomes a little more explicable fifteen minutes later when she falls to the floor where she remains for about ten minutes – while her companions drink unconcernedly on. The crew seems extremely well and cheerful – the omens are good.

Before we all join the girl on the floor I drag Isaac off to a restaurant in order to discuss an idea for a book that I've had. My new responsibilities at the British Film Institute include publishing and at a brainstorming session the day before, I'd suddenly had the idea of Isaac doing a diary of the production. Since then I've thought that I might keep a weekly diary to complement his daily one. The attraction for me is that it will give me an opportunity to reflect a little on my five years of experience producing films. Isaac seems as keen on the idea as I am. I promise to get him a tape recorder and he promises to record his thoughts last thing at night.

As soon as I start thinking about the diary I'm struck by how long we've been working on the film. I always joke that it is five years from the lunch to the premiere. In fact *Young Soul Rebels* will have taken at least that. I first went to see Sankofa in the summer of 1985 and the premiere won't be until 1991. Still now we're one week from principal photography.

Isaac is looking extraordinarily smart – in his new suit from Paul Smith's – and is full of his day at Number 10. I'm struck by how his take on people is so much more in terms of their look and self-presentation than by what they say. I suppose that's the difference between an art school and a university formation.

● Saturday 16 June

Rosemarie was supposed to get me to the rehearsal studios at 12.00pm. I got there at 1.00pm and Dorian Healy (who's playing Ken, the murderer) had already left. I thought he was really pissed off, but he came back – he had only gone out for lunch which was a relief. We then started to rehearse the murder scene. Dorian said to me, 'Isaac, you're destroying my social life with this character, I haven't been able to sleep; I really think he would be different from the way you're describing him.' Basically he made a very convincing case in relationship to responsibility: my responsibility, and his, for the murder and for this character. He talked about how he had been carrying the burden of doing this kind of murder. We don't want to make Ken schizophrenic; we both agreed on that. It's about somebody who can't come to terms with his own desire. He gave me a performance which was really very convincing and, working on it with Valentine Nonyela (playing Chris) the scene eventually became very credible, so we were pleased about that, and I don't need to give Dorian my copy of *Black Skin/White Masks* (Franz Fanon and Joel Kovel's book on white racism) because he understands the role perfectly.

Left the rehearsal room at 2.00pm to go to the production office (which is based at the now-defunct German Hospital at Dalston) with Mo Sesay and Jason Durr who are playing Caz and Billibudd. We only had half-an-hour but of course it went on for an hour-and-a-half which clashed with the other appointments with John Hewitt (the Storyboard Artist), Nina Kellgren (Director of Photography) and Derek Brown (Production Designer) to talk through the shooting script and the drawings for it. Mo and Jason were ready to go so we started the rehearsal and got through the first scene. I explained exactly what I wanted in the Jubilee scene and what it meant when they have their argument after Billibudd has been attacked. We really got through a few barriers. We also rehearsed the scene where Caz and Billibudd are in the car driving. To get a laugh from the audience, the characters have to laugh at the joke themselves really. It's to do with timing and seriousness.

● Monday 18 June

There were some problems last night over *This Week* doing a programme on the conference that Maggie had at Number 10. I was being hassled by them to appear on it. We came to the conclusion that it would be best for me not to do the interview because we didn't know how they were approaching it, that is, whether the publicity was going to be controversial or provocative or what.

Today has been exhausting, going to the dentist first and trying to get my porcelain caps put in which is a deal and a half, and then turning up to the location and doing the rehearsal for the garage sequence, which turned out to be very good. Valentine is a talented young man; he's studying economics at Middlesex Poly and playing one of the main leads in *Young Soul Rebels* – I don't think the two exactly go together. I almost thought today we should just hold the production back by three weeks so that we can rehearse more, but we don't have the time or money – it's hard. Anyway, Nadine and I sat on it for a while. I rehearsed the love scene between Billibudd and Caz, which turned out to be fine. Mo throws Billibudd on the bed, they take each others clothes off, Billibudd gives Mo a blow job and then Caz gives Billibudd a hand job. It's great. That'll get the censors going. I'm going to be looking at *Sex, Lies and Videotape* (Soderbergh, 1989), *Wings of Desire* (Wim Wenders, 1988) and *My Beautiful Laundrette* (Frears, 1985) just to see what it is about those sex scenes that works.

Ben Gibson and Colin (executive producers) wanted to have meetings. They were very worried about the exterior of the garage which I think isn't so much of a problem, but for them it is. They obviously gave Nadine a hard time today in relation to the music – Colin pushing for Simon Turner and me pushing for Courtney Pine. I wasn't at that meeting, but still at least things are getting done. But my main worry is the hairdresser: who's going to be cutting the actors' hair

– we've got to get a good black hairdresser. The hair cuts that black soul boys had in 1977 are very particular.

Got home at about 12.00am after doing fittings with Caz and Chris all the way through the film – different costumes from the beginning right through to the very end. This took from half six to 11.30pm and I've come home and cooked myself Spinach and Egg Florentine which was very nice but very bad of course since I'm on a diet, but still, I won't eat a thing until tomorrow, promise.

It's absolutely imperative that what the lead actors wear is right. There is no archive (at the time of writing) which shows us what black people wore in 1977, especially around the soul scene. It's totally undocumented, so memory becomes extremely important and Joey Attawia (Costume Advisor) has a brilliant memory for the detail of that scene and period. In fact, *Young Soul Rebels* will be one of the first documents. I feel excited about the styling of Caz and Chris, exposing this era on film, but I wish there were more photographic material – we're relying mostly on snap-shots which we're handling with great care, knowing how rare these photos are. Both Nadine and I realise how important it is to draw on our memories of the period.

What else happened today...? Well, after going to the toilet with Simon Relph at Downing Street last Friday and seeing the obvious, and to rehearsals today with Valentine, and seeing the obvious, I could make this diary very Joe Ortonish...

● Tuesday 19 June

I still haven't finished the whole of the shooting script and I really wanted to by now. Yesterday was a demanding, but rewarding day working with Dorian Healy. He demands a lot from a director and we get good results. We did a voice tape for the murder scene which will be used in the actual film as a guide track; it's uncanny. Then I went to Clissold Park in Stoke Newington with the Stunt Co-ordinator, Special Effects Unit and the whole crew. It's extremely difficult for everyone working on the production to imagine what it will be like to film 300 people in a mini riot in this space, so we have to do a lot of groundwork because the translation of images in my mind and how it reads in the script are quite different. A mini riot takes place when the National Front skins and the Royal Jubilee supporters attack the punk concert. We use a little model which is a duplicate of the section of the park we are hoping to film in. I begin to run around like a madman, showing everyone how I imagine the camera movements will be orchestrated. Everybody begins to visualise the scene. I'm surprised by how much I have to explain, even with a model, shooting script and a storyboard, but that's the director's job. The camera crew seems to be getting more excited. Joanna Beresford, the Production Manager, looks a bit more convinced.

● Wednesday 20 June

I have just finished doing rehearsals with Valentine and Sophie (who plays Tracy) and I've realised that somewhere down the line (I think it was going to 10 Downing St) I've got behind in working with them. I had to work hard and help them relate to one another. Sophie was ill today, too; nerves, I think. She and Valentine read their lines. There's an awkwardness in their relationship that I like – similar to the feeling people have on their first date; young men relating to young women. It's charming, but it will have to be controlled. I think things are working out. Well, they'll have to!

I've been looking at a number of films with Nina Kellgren: *Rumble Fish* (Coppola, 1983) – especially the way the fight scene has been constructed; *Mississippi Burning* (Parker, 1988) – to see how the fire scenes have been constructed. There are a few things I can draw upon for the riot sequence.

● Thursday 21 June

6.30am. Woke up, went to see the test rushes with Colin. Arrived at Metrocolour (our film laboratory) at 8.30am. Ben Gibson and the production crew were there. We looked at the rushes and decided that we weren't going to be using the bleach by-pass method which I thought may enhance a period feel. Terence Davies used coral filters with this technique in *Distant Voices Still Lives*, but we found out that on black skin this really deadened the tone. The bleach by-pass made everything that was dark look very blocked, undefined areas of colour – so black was very black. It took out the saturation, and basically saturation was just what we needed for 1977 because it was a year about colour and mood and the colours are important to the film. So we've decided to return to just using the old method that we used in *Dreaming Rivers* (Martina Atille, 1987) – if you want things to be co-ordinated in a certain way, you do it through costumes, through art direction. I think that's a far more successful way of working for us. What happens is that we retain a certain tonal range plus dark skin tones and at the same time we are not compromising the look of the film, colour co-ordination being expressive rather than decorative. We chose blue and mauve as our primary colours.

During the screening of the rushes Ben asked if we could make Davis and Carlton, the two black garage owners, more understandable in relation to how they speak. I thought to myself this is really a mad thing to say in respect of this film. We are interested in the way that Englishness, the English language itself, is being transgressed and re-moulded into something new. Probably, I would resist calling it black English now because my younger brother's white friends take it for granted, this way of talking, this black London way of talking. It has become common usage. In saying this, Ben was obviously wearing his sensible distributor's/producer's hat, but I think this kind of hat he'd be best leaving underneath the desk, and not taking out too often! On the other hand, Ben has been great working with actors. When I went to see him yesterday evening, he spoke to me about some techniques and exercises for actors which were really helpful and of great use today.

Anyway, the day went on and I did my rehearsing with Mo Sesay (Caz) and Eamon Walker (Carlton). In one scene, Carlton says, 'As long as you are giving it to them Caz...' – that old fashioned machismo way of looking at sex, gay sex in particular. He really found it very difficult to identify with Caz as a brother I thought. It's interesting working with actors, because a lot of black actors are not really given the chance to show their full range of capabilities. When you work with them you have to unpack them somehow, which is always very hard work. In the future I'm really going to try to have a much longer rehearsal period (like Mike Leigh), although I've had three weeks which is pretty generous so I've been told.

I went to see locations afterwards, including a crypt in a church in Deptford, which is where we are going to be shooting the disco scene. Nina, Derek Brown and Ian Ferguson (First Assistant Director) came too. After that we all went to see the garage. I was really surprised to see how much work the art department had done – everything seemed to be ready. There are just a few technical problems with the garage so I talked to Derek. He seemed rather upset and told me that one of the art directors, Lucy Morahan, is not well – in fact it seems quite serious.* He's had to call in somebody new to work with him. He's getting skinny and I've really been worried about him. He said to me, 'Isaac, I get

* Unfortunately, Lucy Morahan died on 22 September 1990. The film is dedicated to her.

skinny when you make films and you get fatter.' It's true, I just eat and eat when I'm shooting. I swear to him that I won't get fatter this time. He laughs and so do I. When I'm laughing I realise how well he knows me and how I really can't imagine working on a film without him. I see him as part of the family. He's one of the best Production Designers in town. Both I and Derek Jarman would vouch for that, I'm sure.

Sophie Okonedo (**Tracy**) and Valentine Nonyela (**Chris**) in the foyer at Metropolitan Radio

● **Friday 22 June**

In the afternoon I did some work with Sophie and Valentine. I think they seem to be relating to each other better, even in the love scene. However, there is this thing about them being uncomfortable with each other but at least they are acting together which they weren't doing before. I'm still worried about it; I must take them out for dinner.

We were going to use the *Daily Express* building for the entrance of Metropolitan Radio Station, but it fell through, so now we'll have to revert to using the civil engineering building which is situated just off Parliament Square – it's very different. I found it quite hard to adjust after doing the shooting script and being prepared to use a space which we are not using anymore. Also, I had to go back to the rehearsal rooms. I found Dorian Healy had been waiting for me for about an hour and a half – he seemed to be agitated and I apologised. It was very strange; Nadine was sitting down cruising the boys while they tried on different costumes (they have to look right, don't they?). Poor Dorian had to change with everyone sitting around looking at him (but he *is* good-looking). I'm guilty too. I had to tell Annie Curtis (Costume Designer) to stop dressing Billibudd as if he's on a cat walk. I want him to be a genuine character, not just a fashion model. Annie just gets excited, I guess, but to tell you the truth, so do I. They all end up looking really great. *Vogue*, eat your heart out.

Saturday 23 June

Dorian Healy and I spent some time reworking the murderer's confession – I really think we've cracked it. So I think we're made his confession more believable. It puts a lot of onus on Chris but I think it really works and is more convincing.

Sunday 24 June

Yesterday I was working on the shooting script with John Hewitt and Derek Brown, doing the story board for the riot scene in the park – the one that everybody's worried about. John Hewitt had the brilliant idea of bringing along some model cowboys and indians (the imperialist Hollywood cliche). So, I laid out cowboys and indians in all the different places that I imagined people would be for the concert. Then Derek got out a drawing and relief plan of the stage. I was eating strawberries and we used some to stand in as trees and bushes. We moved strawberries and cowboys and indians across the table, and for the first time Derek and John finally understood what I was talking about in relation to the actual scenes, camera movements and positioning of subjects in the frame. Everything seemed much clearer. At last I'm no longer talking to myself.

I really desperately wanted to get my hair cut. For the first day of shooting I believe it's very important for the director to look smart if he or she is supposed to carry the currency of authority. Anyway, I went to get out of the BFI Production offices and found I had got locked in. I wasn't given the right set of keys, so it was quarter past four by now and I was stuck in BFI Production on a Saturday! Luckily I was able to change my appointment for the hairdresser. Derek rang up Sarah Gater (Cost Controller for Film on Four) because we knew there were a couple of people from the *Young Soul Rebels* production who were going to see her that afternoon to go through the final things for Channel 4. So, Sarah came, we got out, I had my hair cut and I felt better.

I went to buy a few things for my friend, film-maker Steve Farrer, because it was his birthday, and began to start on the shooting script again. I was meant to go to Hampstead Heath for Steve's 'picnic party'. Rang up Steve to see if it was still on, just to check. He told me, halfway into our conversation, that Atilio Lopes had died. Atilio used to be one of the main dancers in the Lindsay Kemp Company and he's been ill for quite a long time now, the best part of two to three years. Over the last year, on several occasions, we thought he was going to die. For some reason it just totally caught me by surprise, I was just utterly dumbfounded, silenced, and I just didn't really say anything. I definitely couldn't do any more work. I told John Hewitt to go home and packed all my stuff up at the BFI and went over to see Steve and Sasha Craddock (art critic for *The Guardian* and long-time friend). We just talked about Atilio and got drunk. Anna Thew (experimental film-maker) joined us. I'm fed up with people dying from the big 'A'. I'm angry, very angry. I've got to make a good film for Atilio.

◆ **Friday 22 June**

I go down to talk to John Wilson, the editor – I am suddenly concerned that not enough attention is being paid to the sound. When you see the crew credits on Hollywood films you realise that they have almost as many people working on the soundtrack as the picture. I think that there is a systematic neglect of this area in European pictures and I suddenly realise that it's not an

*John Wilson (editor) and
Zane Hayward (Dubbing Editor)*

area which I've discussed at all with Isaac. I'm a fanatic of direct sound and I'm absolutely appalled when I find out from Nadine that most of the music scenes are going to be shot without music. There are, of course, good reasons for this – the more you use direct sound, the more you are likely to make for horrendous problems in the editing. Sankofa obviously had a bad experience on *Passion of Remembrance* and don't want to repeat it. I'm furious – partly with myself for not having thought of this earlier and partly with Nadine who treats me like a simple-minded and rather ignorant child who doesn't understand the business of film-making.

There is probably nothing I find more annoying about film-making than the fact that it is full of people telling you things can't be done on the basis of their own particular experience. There are technical constraints but they are much, much rarer than most production people allow. Whatever the real possibilities, it is far too late to change the production plans. My worries are now multiply-

ing. Ideally I would like everybody who is going to be involved with the sound-track to be in place by now so that a detailed discussion could be going on with the sound recordist to see what sound he would need to pick up in addition to recording dialogue. Isaac, though, has resisted choosing a composer, so I content myself with talking to John Wilson and making sure that he will brief Ron Bailey (Sound Recordist). However, I feel extremely angry with myself for letting us get into this situation.

By this time in a production, however, it's difficult to tell what is real and what is not – everybody is very nervous and I find it difficult to be sure how far my own worries are justified.

The general nervousness had come out yesterday at a screening of some tests. Isaac was trying to get some distance into the image with filters and the by-pass process we used on *Distant Voices Still Lives*. In fact, the untampered image looks great but draining the colour out or emphasising the reds or blues looks silly. In the course of the discussion Ben suddenly tells Isaac to tone down the 'I and I' language of the brothers. I am really furious – along with my obsession

*Valentine Nonyela (**Chris**)* →

*Setting up tracking shot for **Chris***'s entrance into ***Carlton***'s garage*

*Setting up steadicam shot of **Davis** entering garage*

with direct sound is an obsession with hearing the voices as they are – not dubbed into mid-Atlantic. Anyway, the whole point of the 'roots' language is that whitey can't understand it. Isaac doesn't seem phased by it but later he tells me that he's very upset. I tell him not to worry but then have to worry myself about whether there's going to be a lot of conflict with Ben. It's potentially a difficult situation with my last project being Ben's first. To date, everything has worked very well, with Ben really improving the script and putting in a lot of work to raise the German money, but perhaps now it is all going to turn nasty. I console myself with the thought that everybody is incredibly jumpy. It's actually a minor miracle that any film reaches the screen. We're a week from the start of the shoot and nothing miraculous has yet happened. Two weeks in, we'll all feel better.

As I leave the production office I bump into Mo and give him a lift to the rehearsal rooms – he's very downcast because he's just failed his driving test. He also tells me that he's already had a lot of arguments from black friends about playing a gay character. I knew in an academic way that many blacks see homosexuality as a white man's disease which doesn't affect them but Mo's worries make me realise that this is going to be a major problem. The crucial thing about sex in this movie is that it is mixed – mixed colours, mixed genders; to talk about it as a gay movie is completely wrong, but we actually need a new term for it. Whatever that will be will also cover Hanif Kureishi's work, which this movie is related to. Funnily enough Kureishi is currently casting for his first movie as director – and is seeing a lot of our actors. Isaac's attitude to Kureishi is fairly ambivalent. He admires him a lot but obviously doesn't want to be too identified with him. He doesn't like it when I joke seriously that they're going to be seen as twins – just like Shwarzenegger and de Vito.

● Monday 25 June

The first day of shooting went very well. Our second take of the scene where Ken actually goes for Chris, really worked, and was quite an achievement. Dorian (Ken) was, of course, excellent.

Hopefully, the rushes won't disappoint me tomorrow evening when I see them in relation to the framing and the colour.

There were so many people. I thought to myself, this is why it costs so much money to make British movies. They all had something to do, I suppose, but does one really need so many? Union regulations I guess! At the end of the day I had a headache but it wasn't from doing what I was doing; it was from the continual buzzing from the audience of helpers. Mo gave me a bit of a fright when I saw what the hairdresser had done for him, but it worked out OK in the end.

Today I realised that some of my work actually seeps through. It was amazing to see what I had visualised was there, in front of me.

A hundred cheers for Derek Brown, Production Designer. I'll have to phone him up and tell him. My boyfriend has gone to Cumbria for the week; it's quite

good because it gives me total concentration which is what I need. I must admit that with the shock of Atilio dying this weekend I still feel affected by the presence of death which seems to be everywhere. Nadine's mother died recently too and it brings back all the feelings about my brother Jeffrey's death in 1980. Also Mark Banks, a friend I grew up with, is ill with the

Rehearsing Ken's attack on Chris →

Ken (Dorian Healy) confesses to Chris (Valentine Nonyela)

big 'A'. No one can escape these things nowadays – it's becoming ingrained in our culture. When Ken attacks Chris, there's a connection, a strong sense of death. Film-making seems so insignificant compared to what's going on.

● Tuesday 26 June

I am not entirely happy with the way the rushes look. Basically, I think things are often overlit: I don't want so much contrast, but it could be the way the rushes have been printed. I'm trying to make a film which is, in some instances, dark and moody. On the organisational side, there is a problem of the co-ordination of different departments. The system of command, which should all be directed through the First Assistant Director, has not always been happening and hence there hasn't been the real attention and focus that is needed for us to do thirty shots in a day. At the moment I think we are roughly a day behind, to be honest, which is not that good on the second day.

Yvonne Coppard (make-up) was able to help us to light very dark skin tones such as Mo's, and Jason's which is pale. Dealing with those two contrasts in the same frame is quite difficult. This happens because film is a non-neutral technology, premised on favouring lighter skin tones.

Caz (Mo Sesay) and Billibudd (Jason Durr) outside the park

Mo was on set for the first time today and was great. Younger actors always look good but are more difficult, harder to work with, because they tend to act more individualistically than collaboratively. Still, it's fun, and I'm learning all the time.

Rosemarie sent an audio interview I did with Trinh T. Minh-ha off to her in San Francisco. Trinh made *Reassemblage* (1983), an important critique of ethnographic film-making. I had received a letter saying she really wanted this interview for her new book. I'm glad she'll be able to use it.

I received my principle photography payment and paid some of my debts. I don't really have much left which means that I'm going to have to watch it for the next couple of months...

● Thursday 28 June

It's the fourth day of shooting. Today went very well. I think Nadine and Joanna must have scared the living daylights out of everybody. We actually got quite a few shots done; people really seemed to work a lot better, more efficiently. I saw some rushes which I was pleased with, though I still felt they were that little bit too light, but Karin Bamborough (Commissioning Editor for Film on Four) disagreed and thought they were too dark, so it gets really complicated. The expressionist look that I want and the look other people would like to see are really two different things. Interestingly enough, the film-maker Haile Gerima – the father of the kind of black film-making that I first recognised as an independent black film practice – came to the set today with Maureen

Isaac Julien and Rosemary Julien on the garage set

Blackwood (from Sankofa) which struck me as significant. Somehow, Haile looked worried. I think he's had a very hard time making his films in the 1980s, but he's shot his new film and I'm sure it will do well. I wish him luck and hope he does get some more money from Channel 4. He complained about them, saying that they didn't really give him that much for what he's trying to do.

My mother came to the set today which was a wonderful surprise. She sat down and watched everything that was going on, and what was being shot. I introduced her to some of the actors. We went to Anna's Place in Islington for dinner, which was interesting. She really liked the food, and she thought

Anna was great, despite the white middle-class clientele which surrounded us.

● Friday 29 June

It's the end of the first week's shoot and I think I've just become really excited about the film. I think Nadine and Joanna don't want Nina to operate and light at the same time, so I'm really in a dilemma. Obviously I want to have my film, I want it to be shot, and I want Nina to shoot it. I've been pleased with her shooting.

Soul boy, soul girl, punk girl

We did the final dance sequence today. It really means a great deal to me, all the different races as it were coming together. Some people may think I'm trying to do a 'family of man' number. That kind of criticism of it won't hold because this is really how it was at that moment. I suppose it's the mixing really – there's a white punk boy, there's a white converted soul girl (Jill), Chris and Tracy (the two black mixed race characters), plus Caz. It just seemed to work for me, it's London. The actors did really well, have got to know each other, and now they are a good team.

Dorian Healy had to wait for nearly ten hours today, to do his murderer's POV (point-of-view), going about looking for TJ's cassette recorder, and he didn't even get a half profile shot in. I think he really is a true method actor; he brings himself through the experiences. But I think something else might be happening, to be honest, which is desire... He's not stupid, Dorian, and maybe I've looked at him in ways that I shouldn't have done. I'm not saying that I've been overtly flirting but, put it this way, if Dorian Healy was, I'd have to seriously think about things, I think.

Sophie made her first appearance today as Tracy. She was nervous. The characters are really young. You realise that there's a difference between people being twenty-one and twenty-nine; a big difference. That really comes over, which is good. Anyway, one week gone, six weeks to go, and I'm sure that we're going to look back at the garage and say this was the easiest week.

● Saturday 30 June

Went out with my mother and my friend Mark Nash to the Brixtonian, a West Indian restaurant in Brixton, where we met some people who were on the shoot of the Peter Gabriel Rock Promo I directed for the song 'Shaking the Tree'.

After dinner we went to a party that Sunil Gupta (Stills Photographer) was having for his mother, so his mother met my mother. She talked a lot – she's like a Gayatri Spivak (cultural and literary theorist) on speed, she was great! Anyway, we didn't stay very long and then came home. During the day I was working on the shooting script with John Hewitt and we finally completed the storyboard for the Jubilee party. Everything else seems to be fairly under control. I had a number of conversations with Joanna and Nadine – a lot of pressure for me to have a camera operator... I think we really need another week. Nina needs a chance to see if her department can come up to speed before we do anything, but in terms of the actual shots that we are getting, I'm very pleased. There's a post feminist dilemma here – if you do have a woman who is a very good camera operator and director of photography you should try to be as supportive as possible. But one can see similar problems in the Black Independent and gay film scene too. It's a strange industry to be in sometimes. Theory and practise don't ever fit neatly together; in fact they don't meet at all any more in film-making.

◆ Paris – Friday night, 29 June

First week of shooting completed. I go down the first day and am much impressed by the atmosphere. Ian, the first, is obviously enjoying himself. The crew is really mixed, both socially and racially – much younger and much more street than the BBC crew that is shooting *Hallelujah Anyhow* (the other film that I'm involved with this summer). The rushes the next morning are fantastic although Isaac thinks that they're too light. I don't really understand what he's saying but then I don't have to – what matters is that Nina does. The relationship between director and his or her cinematographer is pretty weird. Mind you, most relationships with the director are pretty weird.

The second day is a disaster – they drop over half the day's set-ups. Everybody is getting at Nina. In some ways this is normal. Everybody blames the camera department when things fall behind because getting the lighting absolutely right is always the most time-consuming of tasks. But what really worries me is that Nadine says Isaac is not even getting the lighting that he wants. What he's getting is a very glossy surface look and what she and Ben say he wants is much more of a chiaroscuro effect with far more depth of field.

There is much talk of sackings and getting a more experienced cinematographer. When Isaac had insisted on Nina to light the picture I had been very torn. I loved the work I'd seen but really wanted someone more experienced. I'd reconciled myself to the decision with the thought that we could always replace her. Now that people are talking about this as an option I know that this was executive bravado. If we sack such a key member of the crew, the film will never recover. We may get all the scenes shot on schedule but the result will be lifeless. On the other hand if Isaac isn't getting the look he wants then we are in deep shit. I've never worked on a film when the director wasn't getting exactly what he wanted from the camera but I doubt that it will prove a life-enhancing experience.

Unwillingly, I tell Isaac that he has to come round and see me after he's finished the recce on Wednesday evening, however tired he is. He arrives very late but assures me that he's getting exactly the lighting he wants. As we talk through the scenes he's shot, it becomes very clear to me that every detail in the frame, the anachronistic mike that Soul Patrol use, the deliberate camera movement in the shower scene, everything is exactly as he wants it.

My feeling of relief is immense. No matter how detailed the discussions, no

L to R: Isaac Julien, Nina Kellgren (Director of Photography), →
Clive Curtis (Stunt Coordinator), Richard Philpott (Focus Puller)

matter how much has been planned – and *Young Soul Rebels* is the most planned movie I've ever worked on – there is a terrible anxiety as one starts shooting that no-one is exactly in charge of this chaotic process. From a production point of view you can fool yourself about your degree of control but when push come to shove, or rather when you hear 'Action' on the first day of shooting, you know that if your director doesn't know what he's doing, then you'd be much better off taking up some other line of work.

◆ **Digression 1: Authorship**

This practical recognition of the vital importance that the film has both an author and an authority may seem to fit uneasily with all these theories that pronounced so definitively on the death of the subject. If my experience of film-making has fed into my theoretical concerns then this is the most obvious area. The attack on the author, mounted most elegantly and most tellingly by Roland Barthes, was concerned to displace the literary concept of a self sufficient and autonomous creative source. The etymology of author takes us back to authority and, in classical terms, an author was not an individual teeming with originality but the name for a text which had authority, a Galen or a Pliny. In the Renaissance, in relation both to the establishment of vernacular languages and to the development of laws of copyright around printing, you get the beginnings of our contemporary notion of an author. John Milton is perhaps the supreme example of this half-new and half-old figure. Desperate to protect his copyright and absolutely convinced of the novelty of his project ('things unattempted yet in prose or rhyme' – *Paradise Lost*), Milton nonetheless looks back to the classical tradition to authorise his enterprise. This new author has still not fully separated himself from the texts or the society that surrounds him, indeed he attempts to be the voice of that new Protestant society. It is with the Romantics that one gets our fully developed notion of an author: the individual, cut off from society, calling on the resources of Nature to achieve this separation and thus becoming his own source of power and authority. It is this notion of the author that is still current in much of our unreflected thinking and which Barthes was so determined to attack. Barthes wanted to stress that all the forms of the language that the author uses from the sentence to the genre, are social forms which articulate him as much as he articulates them. Barthes dissolves the author into the social text that surrounds him. What is historically very ironic is that at the very moment that Barthes, Michel Foucault and others are busy killing off the author, a new kind of author is being born in the film criticism of the *Cahiers du Cinéma* critics, Truffaut, Godard, Rohmer, etc. What is interesting about the *Cahiers* theory is that is stresses the forms that the author is using rather then denying them. The *Cahiers* critics were concerned to challenge the prevailing dominance of the script in French movies by stressing those elements – shot sequence, lighting, performance – which made up the specific elements of the experience of film. In their appeal to an author the *Cahiers* critics were thus concerned to stress those elements which Barthes, from a literary point of view, felt that the concept of an author repressed.

Barthes, however, was concerned with the sphere of high art. *Cahiers'* peculiarity was that their theory of the author was articulated both in relation to the materiality of the form but also, and this is the crucial point, from the point of view of the audience of a new mass art.

When, in the 60s and 70s, film theory was born and attempted to develop *Cahiers'* insights, it did so without using the concept of the author. The problem was that while the abolition of the author did succeed in allowing the analysis of patterns and repetitions in the text which seemed to fall outside any author's conscious control, these patterns and repetitions became very difficult to fix ontologically. The logic of these codes was located in the text itself outside of any consideration about their moment of production or reception. The result was a kind of wild swinging from the freezing of meaning in the text – determined by a series of reactions which had to follow a general psychoanalytic logic (and one then had to cope with the problem that many viewers would simply not acknowledge that these were their reactions) – to a dissolving of meaning into the audience where it became a relativist and subjective feature of any particular reader.

In fact, if you look in detail at the *Screen* magazine of the period, where Barthes' programme was most fully mobilised in relation to film, then it becomes clear that the author was never really abandoned according to the theoretical programme. Stephen Heath's analysis of Orson Welles's *Touch of Evil* ('Film and System, Terms of Analysis', *Screen*, vol. 16 nos. 1/2, 1975) – the single most powerful demonstration of the variety of codes that make up the film text – draws all the formal and narrative levels of analysis together in the moments where the crippled detective Quinlan (played by Welles himself) tries to keep control of his walking cane. When one considers the significance of the signifier 'Kane' in Welles's own biography, then it is obvious that Heath's text as we have it is radically incomplete. To complete it would need an analysis of Welles's own life and his relation to the institutions of cinema.

In that sense *Screen* needed an account of the author to avoid the devil of meaning inhering immanently in the text or the deep sea of meaning simply evaporating into all the different individual reactions to the text. But there seemed no account of the author which did not grant that author an unacceptable autonomy constituted outside the codes he was using. In fact the process of film-making can be used to produce such an account. If one can mount theoretical arguments to show that the written text is not the product of a single author it is very obvious that in films it is directly counter-intuitive to talk of one responsible author. Even a very cheap feature film involves thirty to forty people working together over a period of six months and the mass copyright law and trades union practice that has grown up around film has, as its major goal, the ever more precise specification of creativity – the delineation of areas: design, lighting, make-up, costume – where an individual or individuals can be named in relation to a particular element of the final artefact.

However, the experience of production relations within a film make clear how one can award an authorial primacy to the director without adopting any of the idealist presuppositions about origin or homogeneity which seem to arise unbidden in one's path. If we are to talk of an audience for a film then, at least in the first instance, that audience cannot be theorised in relation to the empirical audience nor the readings which that audience produces. So varied are the possibilities of such readings and so infinite the determinations that enter into such a calculation that it is an impossible task. Indeed, were is possible to calculate the readings produced by any specific film then the Department for Reader-Response would be the most important section of any film studio and Hollywood would be a less anxious place with much greater security of tenure.

Any future audience can only be approached through the first audience for the film – the cast and crew who produced it. It is the director's skill in making others work together to produce a film which is, of necessity, invisible at the outset which determines the extent to which the film will be successfully realised. It is the collective determination to make something visible which has not been seen before which marks the successful production of a film, and it is in so far as the producers of the film are also its first audience that we can indicate a dialectic which does not place the author outside the text but within the process of production. This analysis also provides an ethic which is certainly important, and may be crucial, in differentiating among the numerous productions of the new popular forms of capitalist culture. Those elements in popular culture which genuinely mark important areas of desire and reflection are those where the producers have been concerned, in the first place, to make something for themselves. Where the determination is simply to produce a work for a predefined audience from which the producers exclude themselves, one will be dealing with that meretricious and toxic repetition which is the downside of the new forms of mechanical and electronic production. A further generalisation would be that genuine creativity in popular culture is also to be found in relation to emergent and not yet fully defined audiences.

Mo Sesay and Isaac Julien

The virtue of the analysis provided by the process of film-making is that the codes and conventions are not secondary but are constitutive of the process of creation and that process is one which continually implies an audience. At the same time the director does retain a privileged position within it; it is his or her body, the visceral record of life, which is the constant limit and ground for the film. Without a director occupying this central role, the film will simply fragment into a series of unconnected elements. And it is that reality which informs a producer's anxiety as a shoot begins.

It is this anxiety which my late-night meeting laid to rest. We have an author. All the other problems are soluble. All I need to do now is spread reassurance while others cope with the problem of making up the schedule.

On Thursday I spent most of the day with *Hallelujah Anyhow*. They're shooting the big scenes in the church – and I really want to see them. I'm not disappointed. The singing is wonderful and incredibly uplifting. The choir and congregation astonishing – not least because there are white faces sprinkled among them. One's preconceptions run into the reality of intermarriage. I have a very strong feeling that we are recording an important part of British reality that has never made it to screen. I'm also incredibly impressed by the director, Matthew Jacobs' assurance in handling the large scenes. There is an interesting contrast between him and Isaac. While Matthew seems to live entirely within the world of movies, I think Isaac's obsession with film is always at the service of his absolute determination to record the experience of the Soul Boys in 1977. One of the major ironies about my own involvement in this project is that soul has never been music that has meant anything to me. Perhaps that's why I'm so concerned about the sound. When Isaac came round on Wednesday I had some early Doors on the stereo. As he left I asked him what he thought of it. I've rarely seen a look of such disgust on anybody's face.

After the disastrous Tuesday no more time is lost during the week and there seems to be a consensus that the problem can be solved by bringing on an operator so that Nina will have more time to light. I fly off to Paris on Friday night on my way to a Media Education conference, conscious that I am now incredibly tired. I analyse the tiredness as almost entirely from strain – by my own standards I'm not working exceptionally hard, but these two films represent the culmination of five years' work. The strain is imposed by the knowledge that anything that goes wrong now can't be put right. In pre- or post-production you can take a second bite at the cherry. But if you don't get it right when you're shooting, then you don't get it at all.

Tonight, I had dinner with two university friends. The quiet and peace of their lives seems idyllic; I feel a deep envy of months in which there are no distractions from the elaboration of ideas and the painstaking checking of facts. And curiously at the same time I find new faith in the attempt to create a new kind of research at the Institute – one which grows out of the new media of the twentieth century and feeds back into them, where ideas and images move together.

Tuesday 3 July

Yesterday was not a good day. Probably because I heard the news that my friend Mark Banks has been critically ill. Also Ian, the first Assistant Director, who I'm working with, seemed to be in a really bad mood. He's been really snapping at Nina, so it made the first day of shooting in this second week very difficult.

Atilio Lopes had his crematorium funeral today. I've just returned back from the wake which was depressing and as mad as wakes usually are.

Mark Banks in Key West, Florida, 1981

I think people are just going to have to offer budgets which somehow can take into account the way that one shoots films, instead of trying to take into account television and the way that television copes with how everything should be shot. If we really want that extra excitement around cinema they'll have to pay for it, that's what I think, otherwise they have to forget about all this Union nonsense which I'm not saying in a post-Thatcherite way, but there are too many people that are being paid far too much money on the shoot and the money could be better spent in different places.

Today (Tuesday) we did a *Conversation*-type number in relation to the sound. We had TJ's tape turning round and being re-equalised so we can hear it better in the Caz and Chris scene at the radio station at night. It worked really well.

That's all to report in the diary today. It's a bit boring recently except for seeing Ian Ferguson [laugh] in the toilet (this is Isaac being a Peeping Tom – if you go to the toilet, Isaac will look, do you know what I mean?...).

Wednesday 4 July

After a terrible day of disputes and delays, we went on till after 9.30pm shooting. We got the kind of things we wanted but I had to tell Ian not to use so many extras because I didn't want it to look like *Eastenders*, with your token extra walking in. Although the extras weren't too hot, they looked good. I think it was good for Ian to see the rushes with us, so he'll have an idea of what I'm talking about.

Karin Bamborough looked at the rushes again today and said that she really liked them. This made me slightly worried, though she actually thought they were too dark in some places (the same comment as before), which was good: it means I'm on the right track in relation to it being more cinematic! A number of people have complained about this and I've thought, that's good, because that's exactly what I want.

Nadine seems to be seeing the rushes with Karin Bamborough all the time; she's forging this relationship with Karin. At Channel 4 they seem to want the directors out of the way.

● Thursday 5 July

We have been shooting at the civil engineering buildings in St George Street which is off Parliament Square. A very grand building – a replacement for the *Daily Express* building which fell through. Filming here today has been a complete nightmare because there has been building work going on. Michael Kirk (Location Manager) had been told there would be no building work when we were shooting except between 8 and 10 in the morning, then at dinner time. However, they seemed to be working during the afternoon and they were really messing our shots up. It seemed to me that the owners of the building were very

worried that we were doing this anti-Jubilee, anti-royal stuff. Just because you've got a big crown in the middle of the hall, plus a queen who waves her hand – a cardboard cut out waving model. Chris runs down and bends the queen's arm and then goes and kicks the jubilee crown.

This afternoon it became impossible, and this morning, what with the light going out – a major light – and Nuala Campbell (gaffer) had to ring up the lighting company.

It turns out in the deal that Nuala is doing all these favours for *Young Soul Rebels* because it's not a film with a big enough budget; the lighting company has given us some lights half-price – but obviously deals are deals.

Oh, a funny thing happened today which I must end on: looking at the rushes this morning, Terry, our grader at Metrocolor said, 'God this film looks so good it really doesn't look like a BFI film – it looks like a far more commercial film.' Ben was sitting next to him. I thought this was quite amusing and laughed. So did Ben, but he didn't sound as though he found it quite as funny as I did.

● Saturday 7 July

I had to have rehearsals in the morning at 9.00am. Then I went with Danielle Scillitoe (playing Trish), Valentine and a chaperone to have rehearsals at the German hospital. She was really brilliant, this little girl, Danielle. We went to the estate where we were supposed to be shooting and then I showed her the park. I looked at the locations for the coming week's night shoot, which I think is going to be very difficult, although I'm excited and looking forward to it. We're doing the exterior of the crypt; Chris and Caz coming out with their records, then Caz going off and Tracy giving Chris a lift home. Then we'll be doing the scene between Billibudd and Caz which I think will be quite a difficult scene too. I didn't finish until 10. 30pm and I was so exhausted after dinner that I just went to bed, which means that I've missed Ian R. Webb's birthday party, which I wanted to go to because I really needed to relax.

◆ Friday 6 July

For most of this week contact with the film has been by telephone but this morning I see all the week's rushes which are luminous. Incredibly beautiful (Nina really has done a remarkable job), great acting, real direction. In some ways I don't see that I have very much more to do until the rough cut. The summer seems set fair. I see the rushes very first thing in the morning and then go home for breakfast before heading into the office. I give my eldest son Fergus a lift into his holiday job. He completely throws me by asking me why I have no black friends. When I protest, it becomes clear that what he means (which is true) is that I have no black friends from my school days. I tell him that this is one of the real differences between his generation and mine. The historical pattern of immigration meant that there were very few black kids of my age when I was a teenager and almost none who had been born in Britain. My first experience of black people was in holiday jobs and most of them were older than me – in their mid-twenties when I was in my late teens. If I went to their parties and their clubs it was as that licensed figure – the student.

What I fail to explain to him, teenagers' interest in their parents always being of rather fleeting duration, is that from my own teens and partially because of those direct experiences, I was absolutely convinced that the immigration from the Caribbean was the best hope for British society in the future. When Enoch Powell said that this immigration spelt the end of traditional English culture, I was sure he was right but rejoiced in a new beginning which would allow new energies into the frigid secrecies of English life. When I was

*Valentine Nonyela (**Chris**) and co-writer Derrick Saldaan McClintock* →

made Head of Production at the British Film Institute, it was that beginning which I wanted to see on the screen. I had no wish to deny the realities of oppression and discrimination in our profoundly racist society but what had not been enough said or emphasised was the enormous potential of a multi-racial society. My major desire at the Production Board was to help make that emphasis.

To do that I decided to use almost all our development monies to help find the stories that would do that. At the production funding level there is little point in discriminating, positively or otherwise – there are few enough scripts that demand the immense labour of transforming them into film. One can, however, make a real effort at the level of development – focusing time and money on certain types of stories, certain kinds of writers. This summer is the culmination of that process for me.

At the same time, my son's comment makes me suspicious of my own motive. Am I just another race groupie, leaping onto the only political band-wagon which still has a band on it? I don't think so, but this dilemma merely presents in accentuated form what you might call the endemic ambiguity of the producer's role. If a diplomat is a man who is sent abroad to lie for his country then a producer is someone who takes other people's ideas and pretends they are his own. By definition the producer is working at second-hand serving the vision of a writer or a director. If a producer can choose a particular topic or area, the specific take is always someone else's.

In this case the specific take is Isaac's and his generation. Originally I had gone to Sankofa, the workshop for which Isaac and Nadine work, as I had gone to other groups and individuals simply because they were there. Indeed I had not much liked *Territories*, their first film, and thought of my visit to them as no different from many similar visits that I was then making. What really changed my perceptions was *Passion of Remembrance*, their first feature – an experimental attempt to bring the experience of their generation of British-born blacks to the problems of politics and memory. Whatever its faults, and they were many, it showed real vision and talent. From then on I awaited what became *Young Soul Rebels* with real impatience. When the first draft arrived in 1987, it fulfilled some expectations and disappointed others. On the plus side it recounted a history and an experience – the Soul clubs of the late seventies – which I knew nothing about but which the script made clear were among the first real

Sankofa Film/Video Collective L to R:
Maureen Blackwood, Martina Attille, Nadine Marsh-Edwards, Isaac Julien   Photo by Roger Morton

Passion of Remembrance, 1986

examples of our new multi-racial society. At the same time the script read more like a sociological tract than a story.

The problem of film-making is that truth does not come in a narrative. The images which really bring another's experience to us have everything to do with lighting, design, performance but they have little to do with stories. A story is merely a hook into these images and the trick is to find a story which aids rather then obscures truth. Often, if not invariably, it is direct experience which enables a writer to find such a story. If one starts with the imaginary all one can ever copy is other fictions but if one starts with resistant elements of reality then one can weave a new kind of fiction. At our script meeting after the first draft, I was making the contradictory point that they needed something much more dramatic but something that came from their own experience, when Derrick Saldaan McClintock, the writer, told of the day he spent in a room marked 'Homicide' being told he was just the right colour and age to match the identikit description of the murderer of Altab Ali. They only gave up when it became clear that Derrick wasn't about to wear the tragic mulatto cap they had designed for him. It may sound like wisdom after the event but the minute I heard that, I was convinced we had a film. I read the second draft early in March 1988 as I made a visit from my teaching stint in the States. I was so excited by it that I didn't sleep a wink on the plane. Here was the story that would bring fresh images of Britain to the screen. If there were still two years before the film got made I was always convinced from that moment that it would be. In fact the film went through four more drafts and another writer, Paul Hallam, before it reached its finished state. To many, particularly those reared on Romantic notions of the artist, this may sound like heresy. Who was interfering with the pure vision of the artist? A simple answer would be Channel 4, in the person of Karin Bamborough who, as the major funder, kept posing fresh questions. But this is to misunderstand the nature of cinema. The business of making a film means that there is a continuous dialogue with the audience and that dialogue starts from discussion of the first idea. While there are writer/directors whose first draft is almost identical with what appears on the screen (Terence Davies springs to mind) they are the absolute exceptions. Rewriting is absolutely essential.

And indeed the impetus for rewriting was not only coming from Channel 4. Ben Gibson was tireless in his detailed comments and criticisms of the script.

From May 1989 I had taken on new responsibilities in the Institute in an effort to transform it into a real research institute. My responsibilities for production became much more administrative and Ben became the new Head of Production. It was agreed, however, that I would continue to work closely on *Young Soul Rebels*. But Ben was equally concerned that his first major production should be a success and the last couple of drafts were written largely in response to his queries and concerns.

● Monday 11 July

6am – I've just finished my night shoot of the sex scene, or should I say love scene, with Chris and Tracy, which didn't go at all well. Something rather stupid happened: the storyboard artist did some drawings of the love scene but they were really animated. As soon as I saw them I said to Rosemarie, 'Please stop all distribution of these drawings; they must not be seen by any of the cast and crew – especially Sophie.' Sure enough, the hairdresser got hold of them and showed them to Sophie, who had been at an interview with Hanif Kureishi for his new film *London Kills Me*. Sophie was in a bad mood I think; she didn't feel she did very well in her interview with Hanif. Then, seeing the drawings really freaked her out.

Today, doing the scene for the entrance of the gay club was quite exciting. David Harrison, an artist friend, was amazing as the blond queen. People were thrilled to be in it, although shooting it with the steadicam camera was difficult. In the end I had to shout because things seemed dissipated.

Shooting the roof scene, where Caz and Chris put up their aerial for a broadcast, Clive, the Stunt co-ordinator, appeared to be worried. He asked me if I really wanted the shot when Chris nearly falls off the roof. Dealing with such questions when preparing for a night shoot is not easy. I suppose it's just really demanding doing scenes at night, specially when the night is not that long – it starts at about 9.30/10.00 pm and it's light by 4.00am, so you literally have about six hours of night which doesn't give you much time to get all your shots in.

One of the main problems that have occurred this week is that we haven't had enough time to recce locations so we're having to decide things too late in the day in relation to what we're doing in those locations. Each poses a problem

*Valentine Nonyela (**Chris**) and Sophie Okonedo (**Tracy**)* →

of its own, but at the moment what seems to be happening is that the production problems are paramount and they are overshadowing artistic and creative concerns. I'm also finding it quite difficult to communicate with the First AD who seems to have this very televisual mentality about what we should be doing and how quickly we should be going – he's really not used to making the kind of cinema that I'm interested in.

● Tuesday 12 July

Have now completed the third week. Looking back , the nights don't seem as bad as I thought they would be. Talking with people today, I gather that having to make everybody wait on Monday for the tracking shot of Chris and Caz coming out of the disco at night was worth it. Also shooting the scene with Caz and Chris on the roof with the film running out because the camera department didn't order enough stock, or didn't bring out enough with them on that day was

*Valentine Nonyela (**Chris**) and Mo Sesay (**Caz**) on the roof-top putting up the aerial for Soul Patrol, their pirate radio station*

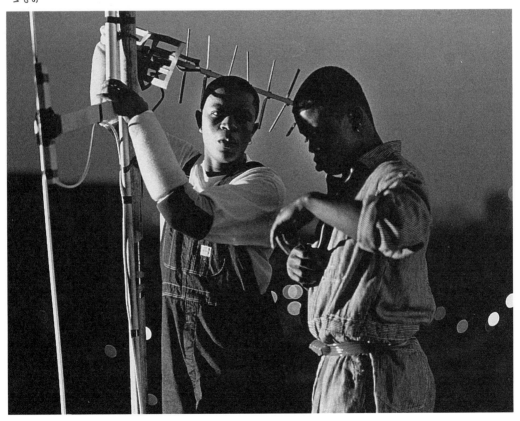

unfortunate. Then we did quite a lot of shots. But what I realise when shooting is that I have to compromise on the number of set-ups, i. e. camera positions, that I want because of the lack of time. For example, this evening, we had six shots to do in one location and five in another, but in reality I ended up doing three shots in one location and three in the other. This happens all the time, so what a director has to do is to incorporate several actions in fewer shots. I have an anxiety sometimes about the way I'm compromised in this. I believe that the

way I originally constructed these shots would be filmically more interesting, but it's a challenge for the director to think on the spot. There's always a shooting script and a storyboard, but these are only guides. Sometimes – although it's always a bit of a risk – when a number of shots are incorporated into one shot, it really works and it is terribly exciting. At the end of the day everybody's pleased with the footage they have seen so far.

Wolfgang Rainer and Ben Gibson

Paul Hallam, the writer, seemed ecstatic today, Colin MacCabe looked pleased and so did Wolfgang Rainer (from Kinowelt).

◆ Sunday 15 July

My desire to drop the rushes comes to nothing. Isaac seems particularly keen that I should see them. Whether he is just being polite, or whether he really wants my advice, I don't know. Early in the week he's been worried about the sex scene with Chris and Tracy. Bits of it are very good but he may be right that it doesn't have enough charge. But there is almost no chance of going back and reshooting it. The crazy logic of film finance means that it is almost impossible to re-do work. The only person I know of who makes films sensibly is Woody Allen. He shoots his movie, goes into the editing studio for a couple of months and then comes out and reshoots the bits that don't work. But Allen is one of the few directors with a track record that enables financiers to agree to these conditions and he works with an ensemble of actors and technicians who are happy to oblige. Perhaps in ten years' time Isaac and I will be working like that.

I also try to think about sex in movies but give up because it's too difficult. In some ways one shouldn't bother because a) it's objectionable and b) it's impossible. But in another way it's crucial because a) it's pleasurable and b) it's vital. This is not a paradox I'm going to solve today.

● Monday 16 July

The fourth week of the shoot. A very slow start. Nadine and Joanna seem rather concerned, but still walk around joking with everyone and generally seeing that everything is under control. Nadine and I had our usual chat in the car this evening and I said to her that if there were really a big problem, I would be the first person to say so and I do think that the kind of things that we've filmed so far have been great. We exchange gossip about who fancies whom on the set. I really value the close relationship I have with Nadine and I couldn't have made this film without her; it's something we've both always wanted to do.

There have been some shots that have had to be dropped but I don't see them affecting the film we're making. I was made to do a shooting script by Ben Gibson. Karin Bamborough never needed a shooting script, I found out later, which really annoyed me; it was just Ben's idea. The storyboard is really what I work by when I'm shooting (the shooting script is too wordy and not visual). At the same time I can thank Ben for making me do the work because at least I can see what shots I want.

Everybody seems to be focusing on the riot scene (most probably because that's where all the money is); people are nervous because nobody's that experienced at shooting these kind of scenes so I think it's about time that we all came together.

I want to include here some extracts from an article entitled 'That was the Workshops that was' by Alan Lovell that appeared in Screen (vol. 31 no. 1, Spring 1990). It's an interesting piece, but I feel he's always had a problem with the black workshops:

> The cultural tendency was obviously interested in aesthetics. One of the great attractions of the cultural politics of the 1970s was the way it renewed and stimulated interest in aesthetic questions. But for all the energy and enthusiasm that went into discussion, satisfactory positions were never produced.
>
> Overall the contradiction between an attachment to an aesthetic of

concepts and an aesthetic of deconstruction was never resolved. Even if a film is an appropriate vehicle for exploring theoretical concepts (I doubt very much that it is), how can it at one and the same time explore theoretical concepts and undermine the codes which are being used to conduct that exploration? [...]

Generally Workshops were not substantially affected by these aesthetics. Black Workshops like Sankofa and Black Audio were a surprising exception. Their attachment to the cultural politics of the 1970s gave their films an aesthetic dimension missing from most Workshop productions (though part of that quality resulted from an interest in Black culture – it was not surprising that names like James Baldwin and Langston Hughes should emerge as reference points). Given the aesthetic curiosity and cultural breadth of Sankofa and Black Audio's work, criticism seems churlish. But for all their interest, I don't think films like *Territories* (Sankofa, 1984), *Handsworth Songs* (Black Audio Film Collective, 1986), *The Passion of Remembrance* (Sankofa, 1986) and *Testament* (Black Audio Film Collective, 1988) escaped from the dead ends of 1970s aesthetics. The ideas in the films often lack substance. The politics aren't convincing. And they offer a sense of 'ART' which is irritating and oppressive in the way Godard's later films so often are.

What we witness here is Lovell's own dead-end theoretical position around aesthetics and politics in the 70s and 80s. I think that the issues did produce some unsatisfactory positions but we saw the unfinished business of these debates in the politics of race and representation. If you like, we're the bastard children of '68, the soul boys and girls of '77, the class of '81.

The ideas in the films don't lack substance and the politics are plain to see by all. The histories of post-colonialism demand a reconceptualisation of the debates around aesthetics and politics. What I hope black independent cinema can do is to shed light on these debates and re-ignite discussion which can both develop theoretical discourses and strengthen ideas around what a left film culture could look like.

To declare, as Lovell does, that he doubts very much if a film can be used as an appropriate vehicle for exploring theoretical concepts, is not only determinist but exposes the kind of bankruptcy prevalent in the left when dealing with questions of aesthetics and cultural politics in 80s film culture. He admits that the aesthetic dimensions in our work were what was missing from most workshop

The Class of '81 – BFI Regional Conference 1984
back row: Simon Campbell and Charles Thompson (Black Film and Video Workshop, Wales), Maureen Blackwood (Sankofa), Karen Alexander (Albany Video), Claire Joseph (Black Audio)
middle row: Michael Greenidge (Liverpool Media Group), Sadhna Gosh (Black Media Workers Association), Isaac Julien (Sankofa)
front row: Lina Gopaul and John Akomfrah (Black Audio), Vickus Mathur (Nottingham Film Workshop), member of Liverpool Black Media Group

productions due to our engagement with the signifying practices of expressive black culture, but then goes on to say that the politics aren't convincing! Convincing to whom?

This question of audience address seems to have posed a problem for both white and black critics, as if a critical take on that question of address, and therefore on the question of authorship also, is somehow suspect when blacks are caught handling it. It's as if black film-makers are allowed only to make political statements when they're in front of the camera, and only in established, conventionally acceptable and recognisable formulas.

To try to escape the dead-end of 1970s aesthetics is something of a quandary for us, as it obviously also is for Lovell – like the return of the repressed. What we do now, which I think is different, is that we are not afraid to explore theoretical concepts while undermining the codes which are being used to conduct that exploration. As I discussed in a piece on 'The Body' in *Third Text* (no.12, Autumn 1990), you have to work within and against the logic of fetishism to make your political points in the cinema. For example, the debate around pleasure (most cogently articulated by Laura Mulvey at the time) has shifted in the 80s due to the return to classical narrative – to tell stories which address the desires of different audiences, such as blacks and gays.

In *Looking for Langston* (1989), as in *Young Soul Rebels*, I try to re-politicise the gaze of black and white subjects. It is obvious to say that in both these films I am interested in the way that white males project their (repressed) sexuality onto blacks, constructing them in fantasy as a sexual fetish. It is the gaze that makes visible that which remains unseen, and it is the business of 'memory' (versus history) and the exploration of racial and sexual differences in the cinema for the 'other' that propels me to make films.

Another thing that happened today, is that John Akomfrah and Lina Gopaul (from Black Audio Film Collective) came on set. They are going into pre-production now with their new film *Who Needs a Heart?* and also into production with Reece Auguiste's film, *Mysteries in July*. So the Black Audio Film Collective's films are going to be shot this summer back to back on 16mm, not on 35mm as they had hoped. They have been trying for roughly a year to raise money for *Who Needs a Heart?*, a 35mm fiction of Michael X, and were unsuccessful, most probably for the same reasons that Sankofa had to wait for a year to get the money for *Young Soul Rebels*. Generally, Channel 4 are not very conducive to giving black workshops monies to develop fictions on 35mm. As long as we make sombre documentaries on 16mm they're interested. I can't help thinking that if it wasn't for Nadine and I being attached to the BFI, we never would have been funded to embark on a project such as this one. Maybe in the future, something could develop but I can't really see things changing very much. Institutions just don't want to fund black film-makers properly. This seems to be a problem for the whole sector, because of 'new reality', because of ten years of Thatcherism – everybody is affected by it. Alan Lovell's article doesn't talk about the Birmingham Film and Video Workshop and the boring programmes that he made.

● Thursday 19 July

I didn't make any diary entries over the last two days. Mark Banks died in hospital – another friend; I can't believe it. This was very depressing for me. I

tried not to let it affect my work on Monday but the funeral's going to be on Friday and it's something that I'm having to repress during shooting. I suppose it connects up with TJ's death in the film... Had a big talk with Joanna, Ian and Nina about working methods and practices which seemed to make the day after go a lot better. Sometimes I think people are too concerned about being nice to each other. We have to be far more straightforward and sometimes blunt in talking about problems.

● Friday 20 July

Mark Banks was cremated at Golders Green Crematorium. I was unable to attend which made me feel particularly bad because I hadn't felt I was able to give him the attention that he needed and I really didn't expect him to die so soon. I spoke to his mother this morning and I got the production office to send flowers. We did the last scene on the estate which was originally supposed to be a night scene where Caz and Chris go out. This really should have been shot at night or at least at magic hour or in the evening. I feel slightly stitched up in relation to the scene – because if I didn't do it today there would be no other time to do it and, in a way, not enough night shoots have been scheduled (of course, all to do with working within tight budgets, etc.). It was a very ambitious schedule and I was supposed to do a sex scene with Tracy and Chris too. I really thought that this was too much to do.

On this last day of shooting in the fourth week what annoyed me most was that so many people were just spectating and I began to feel like an animal in a zoo. People from the BFI, *Screen International, Time Out, Evening Standard* – so many people for this Jubilee spectacle, even *Film 90* were supposed to turn up but didn't in the end. I began to question why everybody thought this scene was going to be so interesting. The kind of spectacle that it is supposed to be is not the real angle of the film, yet it seemed to be the angle that everybody was interested in as a media story. I don't know what people thought coming to the set, I didn't really ask them; Mark Nash thought the scene looked very manic, lots of colours and also that it looked poor, which pleased me – it was exactly the kind of representation that one finds in the archive photos of Jubilee celebrations during that period in East London.

Ben Gibson dressed as Elvis Presley which was very amusing for Karin Bamborough. I thought it was good and sporting of him. When I looked at the rushes today it was bizarre seeing all the colour. There was one shot that looked particularly good, of Chris running through the Jubilee flags for the Queen's speech; through the empty estate. It was the first image that I saw of the Jubilee which emotionally signified the feelings that I had during that nationalist moment: feelings of terror, the terror of a nationalistic discourse that says you have to think like us. When I say 'us' I mean the demonologies of the government apparatus and the state system, the British patriotic sentiments of Englishness. There is a way in which those feelings couldn't be questioned and yet they were questioned. That's what punk rock was all about and that's what being into soul and reggae was about. It was questioning those types of representations. It was the image which I shot of the Jubilee that I felt particularly pleased with. I think one of the most pleasurable moments of filming the Jubilee was Frances Barber coming on to the set; she looked exactly how I imagined Ann to look and was really so professional. She'd only been in London for twenty hours – she flew straight from Dominica from Horace Ové's shoot and it seemed to me that she'd had a bit of a harrowing time being there. She just did

Ann to a 't'. A joy to watch.

Today it was so bright that Mo's face was being totally blacked out and so was Valentine's, so we had to use quite a lot of light and the light that we needed to use was powered by batteries so it just became a real problem. During the shot of Chris and Caz in the car, the riggers could be seen moving about in the background. Ian got really fed up and asked what the hell they were doing. Before he left, he announced that there's a joke at the end of every shoot of every week and that this day had been one of them. He always seems to do it when Joanna and Nadine come on to the set because as the AD he feels pressurised I suppose. Basically, I think an AD has got to respect everybody else in the crew to get respect back. A crew can be easily demoralised, especially on the last day of the week when everybody is getting tired and fed up. Thank God it's Friday.

◆ Friday 20 July

On Thursday morning we see a showreel together with Kinowelt, the German distributors, and most of the production division. Their wishy-washy response suddenly reminds me of how isolated one can feel in the middle of a production. Courage is the crucial quality at this moment – the guts not to back down or begin to temporise.

I'm suddenly reminded of my Cannes speech. This epic discourse (sic) was delivered a year ago in May 1989 as I gave up the Head of Production job to take up my new post at Research. Flushed with the success of getting the only two British films (*Venus Peter* and *Melancholia*) to Cannes and in a tired emotional state, I made the fatal mistake of trying to speak the whole truth and nothing but the truth. While I wanted to thank my fantastic staff who I loved dearly and who work all hours of the day and night, I also wanted to let them know how isolated I felt as *Venus Peter* went over budget, as everybody but me thought *Melancholia* a disaster, and as *Play Me Something* languished in the editing room. I thus committed two cardinal errors. Never use a public event to say something you should say in private. Don't expect other people to do your job for you. Basically you get paid to be isolated and you shouldn't whinge about it.

The reactions to the showreel take me back to that moment and if I still regret upsetting them, I am reminded of how they upset me. I also remember that night because it was the moment at which Simon Relph of British Screen confirmed that I couldn't persuade him to provide the last £100,000 of the budget which we needed if we were to shoot the film in 1989. So tired and emotional was I at this point, and so disappointed at having to postpone the film for a year, that I nearly punched him. One can judge my state by the fact that I am constitutionally non-violent, a terrible coward and half Simon's size. Luckily Nik Powell (of Palace Pictures) and Tim Bevan (of Working Title) pulled me away from the table and led me off to the Petit Carlton where I fell further into tears and unconsciousness.

Thursday evening I go to the wrap party of *Hallelujah Anyhow* and then onto the set of the film where they are shooting the nightclub exteriors. The atmosphere is very good – Ian Ferguson is really enjoying himself. When he was first appointed I'd been worried that such an experienced first might find it difficult working with the off-beat collection of crew we'd assembled, but he's taken to it like a duck to water. The film is getting everything it needs. A lot of needle between Nina and the production office but otherwise fine. I start suddenly thinking about the fact that there may not be an audience for the film and also about whether plot and dialogue will work. The fact that the rushes are great tells us that lighting, design and performance are working – but whether this will gel into plot and character we won't know until the rough cut. I also wonder whether John Wilson (the editor) is going to have enough of a view to give another take on the material. I'm also convinced that the sound has been done wrong. All this may sound as though the film is doomed – actually it simply tells you how many variables are in place. Whatever happens now it won't be an embarrassing disaster. The great rule is that nobody knows anything.

It's been a very easy week. Wonderful weather. The Jubilee party in blazing sunshine. I, for the first time, am paying the penalty of not keeping this diary on a daily basis – I can remember little apart from some terrible performances from the extras. One of the reasons Hollywood films are so good is that the performances are spectacular all the way down the cast list. As if to make the point, Frances Barber is magnificent as Ann, Chris's mother. I'm delighted that I asked her to do it and very grateful that she accepted what is a relatively small part. She's one of those great actors who is generous to new talent and delightfully unpretentious.

Jason Durr (**Billibudd**) and the Pearly King and Queen at the Jubilee party

Frances Barber (**Ann**) and Isaac Julien

Isaac is really enjoying himself. Throughout the film I've been more and more impressed by his determination and vision. He is absolutely focused on recording what mattered to him in these soul clubs of 1977. It strikes me once again that the practice of film-making solves one of my abiding theoretical problems: it is impossible not to think of film (and indeed the novel) without reference to realism. But the great argument against simple realism is that (like Romantic author) it ignores the forms of representation – the fact that reality never comes to us *tout court* but through a very complicated series of practices and genres. To concentrate just on the practices and genres, however, ignores the fact that they are of little interest without an external reality on which they work. The key term to solve this problem is once again a notion of an audience. What is important about what Isaac is doing is that he is making available to a national audience a reality about which it (as indeed I) knew nothing. His success in turning biography into history – in making his own personal experience count within the central records of the society (and this success is not just dependent on finishing the movie but on its subsequent distribution) – will exactly be the extent to which he succeeds in making his experience real to those who did not experience it. The problem with theories of realism and anti-realism is that they have only two terms (reality and representation) when they need a third – how a representation forms a reality for an audience. The virtue of such a triadic account is that it enables us to give an account of two central and common reactions to realist art: that it enables us to see things anew (I lived in London in 1977 but now I see it differently) and that there are often serious disagreements about realism (if the film is successful there is sure to be a great deal of controversy, particularly over its representation of black homosexuality).

In some ways it may seem ridiculous that I am working on a film about black working-class kids in the late seventies. In another way that is the real kick of film-making. It gives you the real chance to work in very intense situations with people from very diverse backgrounds. The complementary down is that the making of the film comes to an end and you all disperse and you know that without the material of the film it will be next to impossible to sustain what are genuinely close friendships. But even that sorrow has a silver lining: at the end of each film, as well as a list of people who you would really like to work with again, there is another (hopefully shorter) list of people who you will never again work with under any circumstances.

Frances Barber (**Ann**), Mo Sesay (**Caz**) and Valentine Nonyela (**Chris**) →
in **Chris**'s bedroom

● Monday 23 July

I've started the fifth week of shooting. Today's shoot went quite well although we were twenty-five minutes late in starting. We don't have enough hours in the day. I'm worried about the two things we're going to be shooting on Wednesday and Thursday because you really only have six hours of night during these summer months. I met John Wilson (the editor), who has also cut all of Peter Greenaway's movies, and saw a rough assembly of the garage, which to me looked really good.

I'm going to go to bed now. I just feel totally insane, I can't keep the diary, can't keep any narrative or logic to this.

● Wednesday 25 July

The first night shoot of the riot went very well apart from using the lunar-crane camera which is very frustrating because you can't actually look at your shot while it's being taken. You can look at it on the monitor but there's no way of looking through the lens which I really think you have to do. There seemed to be a lot of people (well there were 350 actually), including *Time Out*. The oper-

Shooting the 'Stuff the Jubilee' punk concert

ation was successfully co-ordinated by Michael Kirk, the location manager, and I have to say that the real event looked far more spectacular than the actual filmed version. Ian Ferguson really panics when it comes to doing crowd shots – he seems to lose his bearing. I had to organise the last shot myself, in terms of positioning people, and getting people to walk to camera. It was really hard work. The most important shot for me in the film turned out to be the most frustrating to shoot. The shot starts at the barrier at the front of the concert. We see people's legs against the barrier. The camera then ascends above the heads in the crowd; we see Tracy and Chris, and then the camera rises to the highest point it can go, keeping in frame most of the crowd to make it look like a packed concert. We begin to see skinheads attacking people. But the shot didn't work in terms of how I envisaged it. Also, in relation to lighting, I wanted to have some spot effects, similar to those in the dance scenes in *Looking for Langston*, where you get away from realist lighting but adding excitement. I think the concert looked too dark; it was a very difficult shot to do.

● **Thursday 26 July**

We've just finished shooting the last scene of the riot and I must say that I have really enjoyed tonight. It's been glamorous in a way, having to run from one set to the other (we decided to shoot two units in tandem). Unit Two was shooting all the fire, special effects stuff. Joanna and Nadine made the right decision; what it enabled us to do was get it all in the can. There was a kind of energy there, all of the actors were performing very well. Going to the second location, where a fire breaks out on the stage, I remember getting out of the car and seeing Dorian Healy fall into this fire. I was so unnerved. I think all the actors felt nervous that I wasn't there directly directing, and I remember thinking that if anything happens to Dorian, I won't be able to forgive myself; at the same time I really admired him for his bravery, concentration and commitment to the character. He said afterwards that he did it for Nadine and me; he had vowed he'd never work with fire again. Seeing all the rushes (they had all been video-recorded so I could see them on the playback as soon as I got there) I realised the framing wasn't exactly how I would have done it if I'd been directing the shot myself. The shot that I really enjoyed doing the most was with Tracy and Jill standing next to a tree and people running past. There's something really exciting about people running across the frame in foreground and background;

Punks and anti-Jubilee concert-goers →

there was a kind of wildness to it. It was my most exciting day of the shoot, when I felt that we got the most work done. All the actors performed brilliantly and I'm extremely proud of the whole cast and crew. We did it!

● **Sunday 29 July**

Yesterday a leaving party for Kobena Mercer (black media theoretician) was held at my house. He's going to teach in Santa Cruz with Victor Burgin and Teresa de Lauretis. It was a very successful party; I think everybody really enjoyed themselves, but it was a mad thing for me to have to do – I was really tired after shooting the riot scene. A number of people had said that they would contribute to the party expenses and be there helping out as I'd said that I couldn't host a party and do all the work. I had to arrange for some cleaners to come round – the house was untidy because of my working on the film. Kobbie came late and other people who said they would help came late too. When Kobbie arrived I really lost my cool and said, 'Where have you been? It's really late and I'm really pissed off.' Kobbie was rightly defensive about it and didn't like the fact that I'd yelled at him. The party started at about 3 pm and didn't finish until 3.30am. Kobbie said I never really relaxed and tried to enjoy the party. He seems to be burning a lot of his bridges by going to Santa Cruz. He wrote an article in *Third Text* critiquing Paul Gilroy's Popular Modernism debate around black art work and black cultural practices in Britain. Basically, although I found some of Kobbie's arguments interesting, the general tone of the piece I found problematic. Kobbie didn't phone today. David, Mark and I continued to clean up, which was extremely tiring – the garden was really trashed, etc. Looking back, everybody had a really good time (even Judith Williamson!) so I was pleased about that.

◆ **Friday 27 July**

A week of nights in Clissold Park, including the two nights of the riot. I am, as always, incredibly impressed by the logistics. Although I am nominally in charge of this I have no idea how all the components have been put together. The stunt co-ordinator and the second unit are fantastic – I am overawed by the very precise use of stunt skills. The extras look fantastic – this really is London in 1977.

If you thought for two seconds about the complexity of what is being done you'd probably get in a panic but there really is nothing to be done. Once you are into a film this far you have no choice but to really go for it.

During the days the rest of my life goes on. I'm incredibly upset by a meeting with the Race and Ethnicity project. The BBC, who funded this attempt to provide a comprehensive data base of the history of blacks both on and in British television, are now interested in some programmes. The research team has produced a treatment for five programmes but the BBC say they would only want two. The team leader, Kobena Mercer, who has worked with me very closely for a couple of years but is leaving for an academic job in the States, says very bitterly that this is just racist marginalisation. When I argue for their point of view, he implies that I'm much the same. I'm really furious and all the more furious because I can't really understand whether it is just incredible self-indulgence on Kobbie's part (he should know better) or whether I should take as a salutary lesson that however one may be engaged against racism as a white, you never feel its sting (I should know better).

Valentine Nonyela (*Chris*)

● Monday 30 July

We're shooting the disco scene in Deptford today. The Crypt has been incredibly hard work and I feel very panicky about shooting this scene. It is the heart of the film and has to be fantastic.

Although the first day of shooting was difficult we seemed to get through it and got all the things that we needed. The actual posse of disco dancers was brilliant, they were really into the film.

I had a massive argument with Valentine today. He is a very good actor, but has relied too much on his experience of being a child actor. In relation to film acting, he acts very much for the moment and sometimes lacks sufficient resources to deal with some of the complexities of Chris as a character. I said to him, 'Look, what's the problem? You're just not playing Chris.' He exploded, saying, 'You can't say that to me, you can't take the character away from me, I *am* Chris and I do believe in Chris.' I realised that maybe I'd gone too far with him and said, 'OK, I was wrong, but it seems to me we don't seem to be getting through.' I think the problem with Valentine is that he's very clever and in a sense is very confident about what he thinks is right, which is not necessarily what I need. After our argument he seemed to perform a lot better, and it really worked as a shot.

Debra Gillett (**Jill**), Sophie Okonedo (**Tracy**), Isaac Julien, Valentine Nonyela (**Chris**) at the club

● Thursday 2 August

Just finished shooting the last part of the disco scene. Mostly steadicam and we all really went for it. Ian Ferguson was fantastic today, really good at staging people's movements.

Sophie and Jason were getting on really well and I think Valentine and Mo have got pissed off by it. I've also noticed that Tracy fancying Chris just isn't coming over in the film. They work well together on the whole but are not as relaxed together as some of the other characters. Nadine has signalled to me that there is a big problem with Mo. I'm waiting for him to approach me (I hope he does so we can sort this out, knock it on the head so to speak). I'm really surprised by Mo's anxiety about playing the gay role because I thought I'd done a lot of work in relation to making him feel secure about playing that character but maybe I haven't done enough. He's been excellent so far, but maybe the love scene is just too much.

Mo Sesay (**Caz**) and Jason Durr (**Billibudd**) rehearsing the bedroom scene

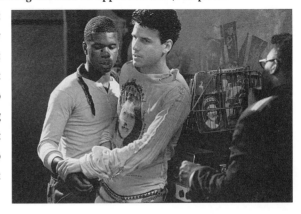

84/5: Valentine Nonyela (**Chris**) and Mo Sesay (**Caz**) get ready to spin disks at the Crypt →
86/7: Jason Durr (**Billibudd**) with his punk mates
88/9: Punk girl and the kissing gay punks, Keith Collins and Johnny Mills
90/1: Soul boy **Irvine** (**Caz**'s friend) cooling off

Ian Ferguson, Andy Shuttleworth with Steadicam, Isaac Julien and Nina Kellgren

Isaac Julien, Jason Durr (**Billibudd**), Valentine Nonyela (**Chris**) and Sayan Akadas (**Asian punk girl**)

Back of Jason Durr (**Billibudd**) and James Dublin

Friday 3 August

Today the steadicam camera blew up! It was very hot, in the nineties. We got the tube station done, which was one of the scenes that we were considering not shooting if there was a massive crisis in relation to the budget. I was delighted that we managed to get it done. We did the last shot in two takes and I chose the second. Everybody wanted one more take but I didn't think it was worth it. Then we moved to our second location in the East End. Mo was supposed to meet Nadine that morning to talk about his problems of doing the sex scene but he didn't turn up. I begin to feel distraught about having straight characters playing gay characters (but Jason Durr's a very good actor and so is Mo Sesay). I began to question my motive for having the sex scenes. Both of these scenes have been probably the most difficult to shoot. Just when I thought everything was going well, this problem with Mo came along and it really knocked me. Obviously, for me, it's important that the gay scene is there. I already felt compromised doing the heterosexual scene because of the number of mishaps that had happened; mainly Sophie seeing the drawings and then the rushes, not liking herself in them, and losing her confidence. The golden rule is: don't show your actors rushes of themselves (although I don't believe this). I really wanted the gay scene to be uncompromised as well. It felt like I wasn't going to get a gay sex scene at all, so I'm really, really depressed about it.

Colin came onto the set today before going off to Italy. I didn't want him to worry about it too much, so I said that we'd sort everything out and see Mo on Sunday. After we wrapped the shoot I did have a long conversation with Mo; he apologised to me and we both really spoke it out. When I saw him again on Sunday, I think he felt OK and the following week it did get better. Approaching last week of shooting now.

Monday 6 August

We've just finished shooting scene 47 (the interrogation scene in the police station). It was a good day: I felt the lighting was good, I got a good deal of concentration from Valentine who was in a bad mood (I know he was pissed off with me again today). But that did help with the police scenes: I didn't try to be too pally with him; his moves were absolutely perfect. We worked with the CID man. I was worried about it because it could be so stereotypical and cliched but because of his performance it's going to be a really tense scene.

Tuesday 7 August

We had to do some night shooting yesterday – I worked with the second unit doing pick-ups for Ken, making telephone calls and doing cutaways for the murder scene, emphasising that the cassette was on when the murder took place.

Today we shot the last scene (no. 45) from the interview room. Henry Louis Gates (leading theorist in African and American literary studies) came to the set today; he had been in London and was on his way back to America. He seemed like a really nice person and was genuinely interested in what I was doing. In relation to *Looking for Langston* he said that he had  spoken to George Bass (late executor of the Langston Hughes Estate) about the possibility of releasing the American rights for Hughes' poems. He wants somebody to do an interview with me for a magazine he's producing from Duke University.

In the evening we did some pick-up shots for the 'Black and White Unite and Fight' slogan because the ones we shot last night didn't work. While shooting this week, I've felt more tired than usual. I must confess that I'm sorry Kobbie's going. I'm finding this all too stressful; I wish he was staying. I feel I'm on my own now, culturally speaking. I wish we hadn't argued.

Isaac Julien and Henry Louis Gates

Wednesday 8 August

We've just shot the sex scene between Billibudd and Caz. It was a big number and took us the whole morning to set up. We rehearsed it with the camera remote and marked out the movements. The first scene went well, but we all wanted to do it again. We did the second take. It's one camera movement and the shot lasts four minutes. It turned out incredibly well.

*Camera rehearsal for bedroom scene between **Caz** and **Billibudd***

*Bedroom scene between Mo Sesay (**Caz**) and Jason Durr (**Billibudd**) →*

Bedroom scene between Mo Sesay (*Caz*) and Jason Durr (*Billibudd*)

● Thursday 9 August

We've shot all the scenes with Frances Barber today. It's a real pleasure to see her performing. Derrick Saldaan McClintock and Paul Hallam came on the set and I asked Derrick for advice on Frances' character. He said she should be tougher while still showing a mother's affection for her son. Paul and Derrick don't speak to each other a great deal; Derrick dislikes Paul because I chose to work with Paul on the later drafts of the script. I don't think Derrick's really being fair to Paul. Derrick's contributions to the earlier drafts were invaluable and we did work well together. Paul doing the later drafts pulled everything together technically; he has more experience than Derrick and his input has basically been the reason why the film got made. Scripting for the cinema is very difficult.

● Saturday 11 August

Friday: Doing the last scenes with Valentine and Mo was murder. But it's over, it's done, it's in the can, it's finished! Everyone from BFI Production, plus the crew came down and we all celebrated with a few drinks. I was supposed to go off to a production/director/producer dinner which sounded boring, but everybody else was going to Pamela's wine bar in Dalston Lane, which seemed more fun.

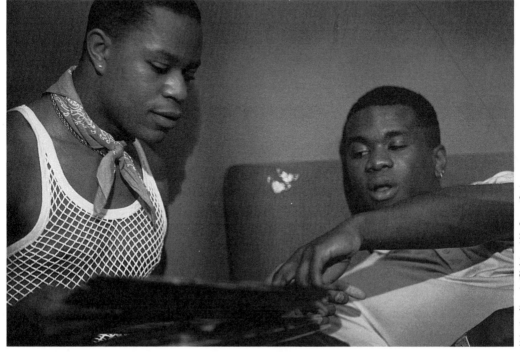

Mo Sesay (**Caz**) and Frances Barber (**Ann**)

Valentine Nonyela (**Chris**) and Mo Sesay (**Caz**)

So Angela Topping (Executive in charge of Production), Winnie Wishart (Production Co-ordinator), Joanna and I all got into the back of Mark's car, drove to Kings Cross and dropped Angela off. We got to Charlotte Street and went to the Italian bar, looked at ourselves, looked at what the place was like and thought, we just can't bear it – it was awful so we ran out. We got to Pamela's – everyone was there, totally drunk and out of it. It's a 'buppy' wine bar, you know buppy/yuppy. Black people go there, extremely well dressed, you know, black professionals. We were in the middle dancing and drinking and people were falling down. You don't really dance in a wine bar, but who cares? I can remember dancing and seeing Ben Gibson dancing and telling him not to dance like that to records like this; it was really funny. Someone in the Art Department seemed to be very interested in Nadine. Zane Hayward (the Sound Editor) seemed to be dancing quite closely with Deborah from wardrobe. Annie Curtis seemed to be on the floor a lot of the time. We just kept dancing. I really thought we were going to get beaten up actually when the bar shut down.

Anyway, it was very lively all evening and everybody ended up going to a party of a Spanish producer friend of mine. When we got there, the party was over. Everybody was really drunk. I thought I'd better get them out. They all went off to another place and I heard quite a few things transpired there.

It's Saturday today, and I'm getting myself ready to go to the post-shoot party. Rosemarie saved the day by getting Westminster Boating Club which we didn't think would be possible.

● Sunday 12 August

The party was a great success (not too much of a hangover), in a brilliant location looking onto the river. It was warm, you could see Battersea Power Station in front of us (one of my favourite pieces of architecture in London). First of all I couldn't believe how big it was as a space – very exciting. Theresa Scherer, a Swiss producer, had flown over in relation to *Memoirs of a Spacewoman* (Mark Nash's forthcoming film). I bumped into her and Mark Nash as I was going in; I was a bit late. I just got through the door when Hanif Kureishi more or less pounced on me; he was with Tracy Schofield (who edits all the Faber & Faber books on film and drama). He proceeded to question me (were all the shoots finished? what was the budget? what was it like doing it?). I told him that the most important thing for me was not putting on 18 stones

← *Young Soul Rebels* Production Posse

which always seemed to happen whenever I shoot a film. He told me how Stephen Frears used to eat a lot when he was directing *My Beautiful Laundrette* and *Sammy and Rosie Get Laid* – they used to throw him Mars Bars. We discussed the actors (I spoke about Jason and how good he was and he said, 'Oh, you mean the Daniel Day Lewis character?' , and I said, 'No, the Billibudd character.'). He was friendly. After that, black writer and producer Trix Worrell came up to me and suggested we open a bottle of champagne. I thought, this is really great, but I'm going on to the dance floor and not coming off it; there were far too many people who wanted to question me and talk to me all the time. I just wanted to get out of it. Everybody really enjoyed the party. Jimmy Somerville came straight from San Francisco. It was like a real media event. Rosemarie had done brilliantly, it was fantastic. I wish we could have more of them. We'll have to make another film, Young Soul Rebels II.

◆ **Monday 6 August**

Colin MacCabe, Joanna MacCabe and friend Samantha Menzies

I spent Monday 30 July as an extra with my daughter. I really am desperate to get into the film. I'm also very worried by the fact I'm going on holiday before the film has finished shooting. The original schedule got changed too late for me to change my holiday. If things had been difficult I would have cancelled but there seems no reason to and I can always fly back if there's trouble. At the same time it makes me very anxious. The soundtrack remains a real nightmare. Everything is in the hands of Still Moving, the company we have contracted to deal with the soundtrack, and although they seem very competent I'm very worried that we haven't yet got all the necessary clearances for the tracks Isaac wants. I think part of my anxiety, as always, is simply related to lack of knowledge. Music copyright is an incredibly arcane and difficult area and one which I've never properly managed to understand. In fact, there seem real questions of public interest which are going to become more and more acute as the years go by. It may seem obvious that a song belongs to the creators and the company that produced it but if it is a song as important as the Sex Pistols' 'God Save the Queen', doesn't it also belong to all listeners for whom it is a crucial personal memory? Shouldn't there be some attempt to limit copyright by money as well as time? When the Rolling Stones have made millions of pounds out of 'Satisfaction', shouldn't it by that very fact be in the public domain? There are very few more important questions of cultural politics than copyright but nobody ever considers them politically. Anyway, these large thoughts are beside the pressing, practical points. Otherwise, everything is going well and I go down to the set on Thursday night (2 August) relatively confident that I can leave with a clear conscience.

When I rhetorically ask Isaac if he's got everything under control, he floors me by saying that Mo is now unhappy about the gay sex scenes, that are the crucial days of the final week. From my conversation in the car with Mo before the shoot, I realised the pressure he was under but the scenes are just not optional. Isaac knows this better than anyone and we leave it that I'll fly back if it isn't sorted out over the weekend. As I drive away I console myself with the thought that as much as anything it's simply actors reacting to the end of the shoot. Actors are in this extraordinary position where during the shoot they are absolutely the centre of attention, because the one thing you can't do is recast once you've turned over. But both before, in the casting, and afterwards, in the editing, they are treated with very scant ceremony. I feel certain that the problem is probably just an indication of the actors realising that they are about to lose the position of power they have held for six weeks.

Nevertheless, I'm relieved on ringing from a French motorway this morning (Monday 6 August) to find out that everything is settled.

● **Friday 17 August**

We left the German hospital today. I feel really sad about leaving it and so does everybody else, we'd got really used to it. We're now in the BFI cutting rooms: Andy Powell (BFI Production's Technical Officer) has done his best – two of the rooms have new carpets and the walls have been painted, but the rest of it looks a real shambles. I think it's a really bad show on the part of the BFI; I mean, it's where all the really important work actually takes place. It is called the British Film Institute and if the Production Department has cutting rooms, I think they should be in pristine condition. I can see out-takes of Laura Mulvey and Peter Wollen's *Riddles of the Sphinx*, *Caravaggio* and *Distant Voices, Still Lives* everywhere. I can't help thinking that in the future people will want to see the out-takes of those films; it's very distressing to see how untidy it's kept downstairs. I think it's a reflection of film-making and the film-making process. In contrast, the offices upstairs look very nice and new as they've been redecorated. I think downstairs should be too. How about it, Ben and Colin?

● **Wednesday 5 September**

Got Nellie Hooper, from *Soul II Soul*, to come to see the film today. He was not interested in doing our film; he wanted to do something more funny, with slightly better money (they had been asked to do the music for *Days of Thunder* with Tom Cruise; I don't think the film is that interesting). I do feel a bit disappointed about them declining to do it because they had the first option, but now I think it's a good thing – I don't think their heads could have got through the door to be perfectly honest. They refused to do the 'Red Hot and Blue' AIDS music programme, being produced by Leigh Blake at Palace, so I doubt if they like some of the themes of *Young Soul Rebels*, i.e. gay stuff. Too bad, maybe they're not so cool after all.

But the coolest guy in town must be Ian P. Hierons (our music supervisor) because he and Bonnie Greenberg (US music supervisor) have cleared nearly all the music tracks on the film. They've done an amazing job (I don't envy them). We are still getting the run-around on the clearance of the Sex Pistols track. Beware! Johnny Rotten (John Lydon) is not what he was. I think he's just interested in money and has made clearing the rights to 'God Save the Queen' impossibly expensive.

● **Wednesday 12 September**

Showed the rough cut to everybody today, well to Karin Bamborough this morning. She was pretty negative I thought; she said she didn't know what happened in places. I know it's a rough cut and not perfect, but I think her strategy in talking about it had something to do with a book rather than a film that she'd just seen. She said that she thought the film should begin with Caz and Chris, which I knew she was going to say, because that's what she wanted in the script and she still clings to this idea. She also talked about the two love-making scenes, saying that they could both be out. I don't think she liked the homosexual love scene – she said it wasn't really needed and that it does nothing to the plot. She can take my name off the film if that scene goes. Neither of them are going. That was why I shot that gay love scene in one take, because I knew I'd come up against these problems. If I'd shot it in a more conventional manner I'd probably be in trouble now. Colin, Ben, Paul Hallam, Derrick, Liz Reddish (Distribution and Marketing Manager, BFI Production), Sarah Gater from Channel 4, Joanna Beresford (Production Manager), Robert Crusz and Maureen Blackwood for Sankofa were at the second screening and they all seemed to be very enthusiastic. I took down notes of people's general reactions to the film and tried to speak to everybody about it. Funnily enough there are some scenes that people think are not very good and should go, like the train station scene. I want it to stay. The Asian woman's performance is a bit polemical, but it was meant to be. Everything seems to be OK and we're working on the fine cut now.

At one screening, Paul Gilroy declared that *Young Soul Rebels* is an 'allegory of the empire'. It's about the 'fall-out' of Imperialism. The characters are residues of Post-Colonialist Britain. It's not realist at all. I'm sure it will get misread all the time; it's not the sort of thing you're supposed to do anymore! I'm inclined to agree with him.

◆ **Wednesday 12 September**

This is always the moment of truth and also the lowest moment of the whole process since the script was first conceived (the second draft in March 1988). The moment of truth because if the film doesn't work now it never will, but also the lowest moment because it is a very rough cut without any real effects track or the benefits of music. Perhaps it's just the day, but I am remarkably unworried. The first thirty minutes are staggeringly brilliant – this is an aspect of London which has never been captured before. The performances are also brilliant – Caz is less moody than I feared, Chris is brilliant as a pain of a smart arse who is also attractive. After the opening thirty minutes, the film begins to sag – all the individual scenes work but, having brilliantly introduced the characters and themes, there is a real lack of focus. I find myself unable to analyse this and the film is good enough for me not to bother but I am aware that a lot of work needs to be done in this area. Then there is the Jubilee day itself. I am completely thrown by the fact that we cut directly from Metro to the pirate station – this completely throws out the narrative climax and leaves one utterly foxed by the time sequence. I also don't realise that this is very different from the script (despite having read it about thirty times) so don't quite see how to put it right. However, I'm soon caught up in the film – each scene almost more brilliant than the last. Funnily enough, the only scene which really disappoints is the large crowd scene (there is no sense of menace of the NF skinheads) – they seem not to have used several crucial shots. But that aside, the film is as good as I could possibly imagine. I'm also relieved, on looking at my watch, that the film has lasted almost two hours. Relieved because I hadn't thought it was remotely that long but also because we can tighten it up a lot. I don't think it should be a minute over 100 and I'd be happier if it were 95 minutes.

There is a good conversation afterwards with Isaac, John Wilson and Ben, which suggests that we're all in agreement on the faults and that the first thirty minutes are the most crafted of the cut. I have no doubt at all that we will have, we have, a brilliant film. Or, rather, that we have a brilliant set of images. But, as Godard has often insisted, film is a question of sound and images and so far we've only dealt with the images. The sound continues to bug me very badly. This is really the one area where I've disagreed with Isaac and the one area where I've really tried to impose my suggestions. On all the major areas: camera, design, editing I have had reservations with Isaac's choices but have been very willing to go along with them and they have all proved brilliant. But I want Simon Turner to do the soundtrack and Isaac has always seemed unkeen. But I really can't think of anybody else who will be able to provide a soundtrack for a mainstream movie which will not be too conventional. I think one reason that I have not been pushing Simon very hard is that I have been worried that Isaac definitely wants a black musician and I just don't know whether Simon is sufficiently interested in soul. Most of my doubts disappear just before the rough cut. At a meeting on the post-production I am appalled that they are considering using contemporary actors to provide radio snippets that one will hear on the radio. When I say that this will sound nothing like 1977 radio everybody looks at me as though I am a complete idiot. I try to persuade them that voice-patterns and styles of presentation vary incredibly over a decade and that as we cannot have any wide shots of London in period, it is through elements of the soundtrack that we will provide historical depth. Everybody continues to regard me as a complete moron and it is only when I start talking about the beginning of *Distant Voices, Still Lives*, where the shipping forecast at the beginning takes us back forty years, that Isaac begins to see what I'm talking about. That, and the meeting with the *Soul II Soul* mixer the day before who turned out to be white, makes me push Simon once again. However, he is now on tour in Japan and I have an hilarious three days trying to phone him. I always get through about 2 o'clock in his morning and he is so drunk that when I follow up the next day he has forgotten what we talked about. However, he is willing to give up his holiday in Thailand in order to do specimens for Isaac even though there are four other musicians also producing tapes. My final conversation with him is that he will phone me some time before he leaves Japan. He sounds as out of it as ever and I am not very surprised that he doesn't. This is the one fly in the ointment. But even this is put right when I get a fax on my return to the office saying that he will phone from Thailand. In fact, he phoned as I typed the previous line and I feel optimistic about his return. One of the advantages of Simon is that he really will design the whole soundtrack.

Second Cut: 19 September

Funnily enough this is the lowest moment so far. I like the film even more, although the end still has a few problems and there is still a slight sag in the middle. But there are a lot of people at this screening and they don't seem as enthusiastic as I would expect. Also, the arrangements after the screening are confused. Isaac basically wants to hear opinions from the people he has asked along; I want a full report on the music budget. I'm now getting worried about the schedule and determined that the final cuts will be made – I don't want the editing abandoned for lack of time. I ring up Isaac and tell him I'd like to spend the weekend in the cutting room. I practically hear him turn white over the phone. With an enormous effort he keeps control long enough to tell me that he doesn't think it will be necessary. I tell him I hope it won't be but they better get a move on.

Third Cut: 26 September

I fly in from the States and get in fifteen minutes into the film. Tired as I am, I am delighted with it. Afterwards I have what I hope is going to be a short discussion, but which turns into a very long one, with Ben, Nadine and Isaac. Ben has taken very detailed notes and insists on going through them – I am desperate to get on and select a composer. Some of Ben's points, however, are excellent, so I leave the meeting and come back afterwards. We go through the five compositions. I'm doing it blind but when we get to the third one I think that this is the only possible soundtrack. However, there is, if it is Simon's, no soul in it. The final one, despite not really functioning as a soundtrack, has some really great music on it. One of the minor ironies of this film is that it has finally succeeded in getting me into soul. The third track is Simon's, the fifth is by a white soul musician, Barry Sharp, who started in the very clubs which are the focus of the film. Isaac, Ian, Nadine and I agree to go for a high-risk strategy which will put Simon and Barry together.

Fourth Cut: 10 October

I have talked to Simon and Barry. They both turn up at the screening. This is the film I've dreamt about. There are two shots I don't like and the riot scene is going to be completely dependent upon the sound, but this is a very good film. Barry is incredibly elated afterwards, talking about the world it evoked. I am absolutely delighted and it seems to me that the sound about which I have been so concerned is now in safe hands. I urge Simon to talk to the rest of the editing team and get back to me immediately. I don't connect with Simon the next day and on the Thursday, Isaac, Nadine and Ian Hierons, the music supervisor from Still Moving, come round. From the minute they walk into the office, it's clear that they're worried about something and what they want is a clarification of Simon's role. In some ways I'd expected some initial difficulty as Simon melded into the team; in other ways I'm very annoyed with myself for not having Isaac at the meeting with Barry and Simon two day ago. Although I can find excuses, there's no doubt that I've alarmed Isaac, and with some justification. He's absolutely certain that he doesn't want a Simon Turner soundtrack which, brilliant as it would be, would not be mainstream enough for the film. I'm equally certain that I want Simon to originate sound and to give the film his extraordinary talents. But I can see I'm upsetting the sound editing team, who have already put a lot of work into the sound design, Isaac and indeed everyone. Anyway, this is my last throw – either it'll work now or not.

Tuesday 30 October

The last month has been incredibly busy. Almost all the projects at the Institute are beginning to happen: the books, the magazines, the television, the postgraduate degree. The films are almost over. If it is impossible to ruin the films completely (the nightmare of shooting), then one can now let them slip into mediocrity. As if to give me a horrible proof of this, I attend at the beginning of the week a post-dub screening of *Hallelujah Anyhow*. Although I have called into the dub a couple of times, I have not really followed it and I sit back expecting 90 minutes of pure pleasure as the sound really begins to do its work. Instead it's pure pain. The sound doesn't seem to be there at all and if the film still manages to work, it is against rather than with the sound. This, which is always one of the best moments in the genesis of a film when it takes its final huge step forward, is easily its worst. Luckily, Bernard Rose (there as a friend) and Mark Shivas (Head of Drama and the other Executive Producer) think that the problem is probably one of projection but I spend a ghastly 36 hours before a second screening proves that this is the case. If, however, one wanted an object lesson in the importance of sound – I've just had it.

Meanwhile Isaac has decided that although Barry Sharp's music is brilliant, he really wants a more orthodox score and Simon Boswell, who did *Hardware*, has been taken on at the last moment. I should feel more worried, but in fact I'm not, largely because Isaac has now really focused on the soundtrack. Up until a month ago I'd worried that he thought the soundtrack was little more than the soul tracks. I now realise I was wrong.

My worries, as they should, have now moved on – I'm sure the dub will go well but there's one final hurdle before finishing the film: the release. We've already had problems over the title. As the designers have come in to pitch for the credits, they are less than enamoured of the title. I've never thought the title was orthodoxly good, in fact it's quite naff. But it is the title of the film. I have an almost mystic belief that films have real names and that you change them at your peril. This belief was crystallised by the experience of a good comedy called *Skin* which I was persuaded, on the grounds that nobody would understand the title, to rename *The Lovechild* – the film closed before the reviews were out.

I have withstood every suggestion that the name should be changed but am now appalled that Isaac has lost faith in it. I tell him that nothing is going to change the title and that he should not bother even talking to me about it. When he casually brings it up in conversation for the fifth time (Isaac gets his way not by being an upfront shit – normal practice for directors – but by persistent and ruthless charm) I finally lose my patience, and with John Wilson grinning gnomically in the background, tell him that however naff the title is, it is the title of the film and that he can't bring it up again. The conversation worries me, however. Not because of the title, which I'm sure is right (exactly what Chris and Caz think they are and what, with ironic distance, Isaac still thinks they are) but because Isaac, when we're talking about the release, starts mentioning *Memphis Belle*'s audience. All film-makers believe that everybody wants to see their films and that it is only a conspiracy of their distributor, exhibitors, and critics which prevents their film being as successful as *E.T.* The reality is that all those people are practising their own trades and have a different view of the film (the critic's being the closest to that of the audience who only think for about five minutes as they decide what to do on Saturday night). The UK release budget of *Memphis Belle* was probably more than the production budget for *Young Soul Rebels*. If Isaac is thinking like this then we are all going to be very disappointed. I tell him that his film has only two certain chances of going to any large audience. One is if we get a hit record as the title track and the other is Cannes. Hollywood lore is that each film is five films – the film you write, the film you cast, the film you shoot, the film you edit and the film you release – and you've got to get all five right to get a film. For Isaac's film to reach an audience its release will have to be perfect and, for this kind of film, there's only one perfect start – it's called Cannes.

◆ Digression II: Cannes

Stay drunk. That is probably the only golden rule for Cannes. Sober up and you might have to confront not only the unpleasant question of who you are but also, and even worse, the appalling reality of what you're doing. The essential primer for any contact with the world of film is Martin Amis's *Money* (Cape, 1984). A catalogue of film production as fast food, fast sex, fast money but, above all, fast drink.

It is not, as many believe, a satire but merely an everyday story of film folk, a record of the axioms of movie-making.

The first axiom of movie-making is when in doubt give a party and at

Cannes you realise that a lot of people are subject to doubt. From the first champagne breakfast of the day to the last disco one is assailed by invitations and the constant fear that you're not going to the party that really matters. There's a rough rule of thumb that the grander the party is the further it actually is from Cannes. This is alright if you've got a stretch limo and a chauffeur but if you're on Shank's pony it normally involves going to some unlikely spot and waiting for a bus or a boat to turn up and take you off into the mountains behind Cannes or out to sea and some waiting yacht. There are moments of acute paranoia as you realise that you haven't the faintest idea where you are, where you're going or why you're going there but in Cannes no psychic state lasts longer than approximately five seconds so the next minute you're just hoping you chose the right party. The trouble about grand parties is once you've made the trip you're probably stuck there for the duration whereas if you're slumming around the Croisette then you can check a party out in three minutes flat.

There are a variety of reasons to go to Cannes other than to sustain an alcohol habit. The first is to raise finance for future ventures – more movies are mooted than there are cinemas to show them. Some producers, such as Cannon, take this to a fine art and have full-page colour advertisements for films which are in fact no more than the hackneyed gleam in some marketing man's eye. If you work for the BFI then you have to make up in energy and enthusiasm what you lack in money for full-colour ads. But although one dutifully proceeds through the day fuelled by alcohol and adrenalin and pitching like crazy, you really need to be a bigger player to make the most of Cannes. This is the world of big bucks and most party budgets here would make one of my films. When people realise they haven't missed a couple of 00s in the figures they lose interest with a speed that to a novice defies belief. The movement from intensely admiring friendship to intensely bored disdain occupies all the time it takes to blink. My favourite experience of this kind came when I was asked by a Beverley Hills careerette ($2,000 dress, expensive perm and working in acquisitions) to explain my finances. I had got half-way through this familiar routine when I was stopped by the lady's horror-struck realisation that I had only a million pounds in my development budget. I patiently explained that the horror story was considerably worse – that was what I had in my production budget – and saw authentic terror precede a hasty retreat.

Talking oneself hoarse trying to interest people in future projects is only part of the picture. Cannes is a festival but it's also the biggest market in Europe and thousands of films are screened there. Situated in the bowels of the huge new palace, the market has little hype and few journalists – just buyers and sellers looking like buyers and sellers. There's none of the manic enthusiasm needed to generate a production, just the sober business of $3,000 for three showings on Yugoslav television. Unlike the multi-digited talk of the Angelinos this is serious business for the BFI. Such tiny deals add up to a large proportion of our script development in any one year.

Finally, however, the festival is about films – the new films, the best films, films from 9 o'clock in the morning till 2 o'clock the next morning. It is only at a festival like Cannes that you realise how much every movie is already interpreted for you – ads, the reviews, the word of mouth, every film is classified before you see it. Not at a festival. Despite the desperate attempts of the producers to programme the audience, and the publicity budgets beggar belief as well as the producers, films are in direct connection with an audience who can make or break them. Here, if there is one, is the justification of Cannes and I hate to admit that I have seen it happen year after year: Jim Jarmusch's *Stranger Than Paradise* (1984), Spike Lee's *She's Gotta Have It* (1987), Hector Babenco's *Kiss of the Spider Woman* (1985) – all were made instant successes in Cannes. Best of all, two years ago, I saw it happen to one of the Institute's own films – Terence Davies's masterpiece of family life in post-war working-class Liverpool, *Distant Voices, Still Lives* (1988).

There is almost nothing to compare with the extraordinary feeling (after a day of heated conversations which remind you how charming and helpful French bureaucrats can be when offered the chance) of sinking into your seat and awaiting the judgment of a 1600-strong audience. The three years' work that went into the film is suddenly condensed into an audience's reaction to 90 minutes. Despite the fact that I had seen it fifty times before, it yields – like all great films – new meanings on every viewing. It was at Cannes that I began to understand the last sequence of the film, which shows the family splitting up as they return to their different homes after the wedding of the last child. We are bidding farewell not only to a family, now irretrievably scattered, but also to a culture, that was utterly transformed by the consumerism of the late fifties. On the soundtrack Peter Pears sings the wonderful eighteenth-century folk song, 'O

Waley Waley', whose complex lyrics speak of the impossibility of understanding love. Suddenly, I understood that this is the director's own statement of the love, both suffocating and enabling, which his family and his culture have lavished on him.

These deep thoughts lasted about fifteen seconds before we were suffocated and enabled by the Cannes audience. The applause never seemed to end. For what seemed like an eternity (in real time probably about ten minutes) they cheered and cheered and cheered. In that period the film moved from being a masterpiece to an acknowledged masterpiece and its worldwide distribution was assured. Such moments justify Cannes but in recent years they happen much more regularly in the smaller Director's Fortnight event than in the Official Competition where the films are increasingly predictable. The old palais in the centre of the Croisette which used to house the Director's Fortnight has now been demolished and one can only hope that the Fortnight will survive its move into the main building.

The really terrifying aspect of Cannes is that all the hype works. For the first twenty-four hours one still retains some elements of reality-testing and the mad spectacle in which everybody is trying to get into somebody else's picture is recognisably weird. But as the alcohol intake goes up and the sleep ration reduces, as one staggers for the second night to Le Petit Carlton where the English degenerates gather to discuss their day of pitching to the American money, it seems like a normal existence. My one great fear at Cannes is that before I escape (and five days is really the maximum bearable sentence), the echolalia and toxic sweats will combine to encourage that most damaging of movie fantasies – the delusion that you know how to make movies. In 1988 I shared a plane ride out to the Festival with Terry Jones who was celebrating the financing of *Eric the Viking*. He amused me with the production traumas of *Baron Munchausen* which Terry Gilliam was then shooting. Despite starting with a budget of $23,000,000 the producer came to Terry at the end of the third week of a long schedule and told him all the money had been spent. The normal round of frenzied and over-excited meetings then took place, at one of which Gilliam broke the round of recriminations by saying, 'Look, I'm the director and my job is to make the movie; he's the producer and his job is to lie to you about how much it's going to cost; you're the financiers and your job is to see through his lies – so why are you complaining?' Pre-Cannes, this seemed both very true and an awful warning of what happens if you leave the world of low-budget film-making. Five days later, as Terry Jones and I fell over each other in the lobby of our hotel at 5. 30 in the morning, I was almost ready to produce *Baron Munchausen* – the sequel. Luckily that was about three hours before I poured myself onto the plane and the whole babble receded instantly from the front screen of the mind into the filed marked Cannes: see zoo. I always feel I'm lucky if I get to the airport before meltdown, but there's no doubt that Cannes could make *Young Soul Rebels* and I spend a lot of time on the phone to Paris alerting them to Isaac's existence.

◆ Tuesday 13 November

Lunch with the Quinzaine director, Pierre Henri Deleau. The two most important sections at Cannes are the Competition – which is the official event and is largely, though not exclusively, for big-budget films and is dominated by complex politics, and the Quinzaine, set up in the revolt of 1968, as a section devoted entirely to the art of cinema. The Quinzaine has been run for twenty years by one man and has much less complex politics. Deleau has to deliver one or two extraordinary films which wouldn't otherwise have reached international attention. The result is that he is not subject to much political pressure. Death for him is if he gives up on his individual taste. Nonetheless I want to bring as much pressure as I can to bear on him. I do not know him well, having talked to him only briefly at Cannes both with *Distant Voices, Still Lives* and with *Melancholia*. I want to persuade him to see the film as soon as possible; if he does not want it, we will need to think of other festivals. Although I cannot press him too much, I assume he is predisposed in our favour. *Distant Voices* was a very big hit for him (and he needs hits) and the BFI is one of the few institutions which is likely to go on producing the films he needs.

A good lunch. He likes food and wine (always a plus point for me) and has lots to talk about. He has the charm of someone who lives on his own terms and outside the patronage of the institutions. He has built his taste into a living and is now largely concerned with building up his television festival at Cannes in January. I'm delighted to hear him say how much better and more interesting television is than film. One of my absolute bête-noirs is the continuous slagging off of television that film people go in for. It normally comes in two versions: a simple kind of snobbery which regards television as rather common, or a slightly more intellectualised version which goes on and on about visual qualities of cinema. Much of the second version draws on French taste for its discourse and it tickles me pink that the wind is changing in France as (about forty years late) they discover television. Of course, there are real differences between television and film. The difference in screen-size really alters the relation to fantasy. The film image comes much closer to the dream, and therefore addresses its audience much more individually than television. It is also the case that television production is very organisation-heavy whereas film very often can operate at arms length from institutions. But this second difference is not an eternal one. The Hollywood studio system was (and is) just as executive-weighted as any television station. But when all the differences have been added up, a great film is almost always still a great film on television and great television is even better when properly projected in a good theatre with an appreciative audience (exactly what the new January festival is designed for). Most importantly, Deleau agrees to come to London as soon as the dub is completed. I feel very confidant we will go to Cannes.

◆ Thursday 15 November

I go down to the dub on the second day. I don't like (or more importantly, understand) the way it's being done – the music seems to come from everywhere and nowhere. However, Isaac seems to have a definite idea of what he wants and the elements – the music (Simon Boswell), the effects (Zane Hayward and the editing team), the musical effects (Simon Turner) are breathtaking.

◆ Saturday 17 November

Premiere of *Hallelujah Anyhow*. The film is screened at the London Film Festival to a huge and widely enthusiastic audience. I don't think I have ever seen a film so warmly received in London. More important, the West Indian friends I have brought along love it. In a way, it makes a very interesting contrast with *Young Soul Rebels*. Although set in London 1990, its focus is a generation earlier than *Young Soul Rebels* with the main characters all having moved from Jamaica to London. It's also more conventional in both story and style – a straightforward melodrama very well told. However, both music and dialogue, like *Young Soul Rebels*, bring you a whole slice of British life which has never reached the screen before. But it is not the mixed race clubs, but the black

Gospel church which we are seeing for the first time. I'm incredibly proud of Matthew, David Stacey, the producer and Jean Binta Breeze, the writer. The night is a triumph for them and I'm particularly pleased that, after all the trouble with sound, Matthew's decision to shoot all the church scenes in direct sound is justified – the music is really incredible. Isaac, who is in the audience, is very generous and seems genuinely to have enjoyed it. For once, a sense of completion rather than of tasks to be done.

◆ Wednesday 21 November

Back to tasks. I go down to the dub (which is almost finished) for a meeting on the strategy for the film's release. The meeting is the most acrimonious in five years. Both Nadine and Isaac are talking about the film reaching a large black audience. I say to them that I think this is widely unrealistic. If the film were as successful as *My Beautiful Laundrette*, with a packed-out West End run followed by a circuit release, it still wouldn't reach a young black audience. That would need a release like *Memphis Belle* with one of the majors putting in a lot of money.

◆ Friday 23 November

The finished film. I take along Fergus, my eldest son, and Roma Gibson, who's editing this book, to get some audience reaction. I am completely knocked out by the film – in particular, I suddenly realise that Isaac's soundtrack, which is brilliant, is the soundtrack of someone who has grown up with sound centre and Walkman; indeed that is the whole setting of the movie. My Godardian worries about sourced sound merely place me in my appropriate age group (i. e. old). More exciting, however, are Roma and Fergus's reactions. They are both wildly enthusiastic. Fergus goes on and on about the film. I suddenly wonder if I'm misjudging it and that there really is the possibility of a much bigger release that we ever have contemplated.

● Friday 8 March 1991

We had the cast and crew screening last night which turned out to be a big success. Everybody who was involved in the film came, but there were some surprises – including Malcolm McClaren (ex-Manager of the Sex Pistols) who turned up with Leigh Blake (from Palace Pictures). The film was shown at the best art cinema in London (the Lumière in St Martin's Lane).

The sound was incredible – Zane Hayward has done an amazing job; in fact the whole post-production team has been good. John Wilson and his First Assistant Editor, Maxine Matts, have made invaluable contributions.

The film is now no longer mine – it has been let free to the Imaginary of interpretation, of what audiences will think. The reactions don't surprise me although, of course, directors are vain and helpless creatures in this scenario. I wonder what my mother and father think as they watch. I hear the crowd laughing a lot and the mood changes during the gay exchanges between Caz and Billibudd – some people are shocked but gay friends of mine are delighted. After all, it must be true to say that nearly all the films I've made with Sankofa have always produced controversial reactions. As long as I can be provocative and keep people thinking through looking, then I feel satisfied. If some are outraged, they should think again because there are a lot of things that I'm outraged about too. We live in contradictory and complex times. The Thatcher years have been cruel and there has to be a cinema which matches that complexity. Sankofa has just been cut by local Government. The British Film Institute's changes in funding priorities means that the BFI is in favour of the transformation of the grant-aided independent sector to what they call a 'mixed economy' – to enter somehow into the market place. Rather, the infrastructure of black film-making in this country is being destroyed because cultural practise is no longer considered important. Because of the crisis in funding, Sankofa's future is threatened as is black independent film generally. I don't want the film, and the fact that I directed it and Nadine produced it, to be used as an 'alibi for success'. It has become increasingly difficult to make films in Britain now because of the government's attitude to subsidising indigenous film culture. It is clear that the film lobby, developed from the Downing Street Seminar, has so far not gained the kind of government support it deserves. The UK film industry remains isolated in its poverty following the recent budget, while the majority of European countries bask in their governments' support. But the reality in the UK for an independent black film group such as Sankofa is that we have been forced to sign on as unemployed while developing new scripts. However, we remain hopeful. We didn't call ourselves young soul rebels for a cheap laugh then, and we don't now.

Isaac Julien signing off.

Debra Gillett (**Jill**) and Sophie Okonedo (**Tracy**)

Angela Noakes (script supervisor), Mo Sesay (**Caz**), Jason Durr (**Billibudd**), Ian Ferguson (First AD)

Mo Sesay (**Caz**), Isaac Julien, Jason Durr (**Billibudd**), Ian Ferguson (First AD)

Isaac Julien

Mo Sesay (**Caz**), Andy Shuttleworth, Debra Gillett (**Jill**), Ian Ferguson (First AD)
and Sophie Okonedo (**Tracy**)

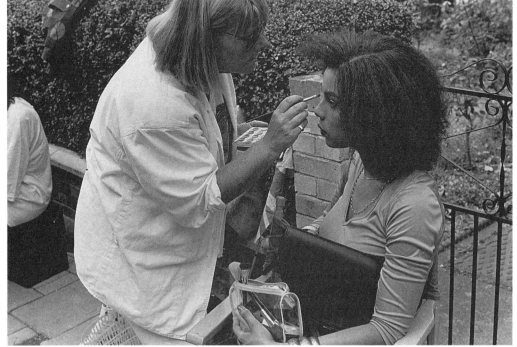

Yvonne Coppard (make-up artiste) and Sophie Okonedo (**Tracy**)

Isaac Julien and Mark Nash

Angela Noakes, Andy Shuttleworth, Isaac Julien and Nina Kellgren

Michael Carter (Assistant Art Director) arranging 'Stuff the Jubilee' poster

*Debra Gillet (**Jill**) and Sophie Okonedo (**Tracy**)*

Production Crew

Mo Sesay (**Caz**), Jason Durr (**Billibudd**), Debra Gillett (**Jill**) and Sophie Okonedo (**Tracy**)

*Guy Burgess in **Looking for Langston**, 1989*

*Matthew Biadoo and Ben Ellison in **Looking for Langston***

Isaac Julien in conversation with Bell Hooks*

States of Desire

Most people know little about contemporary black British culture beyond its presence in popular music. Yet one of the most extraordinary developments in the past decade has been the new wave young black independent film-makers associated with such London-based groups as the Black Audio Film Collective and Sankofa Film and Video, which Isaac Julien helped found. Born in East London and raised in Bow, Julien studied film at the St Martin's School of Art. With the Sankofa collective, Julien directed *The Passion of Remembrance* (with Maureen Blackwood; 1986), *This is Not an Aids Advertisement* (1987), and the award- winning *Looking for Langston* (1989). He has also directed *Shaking the Tree* (1989), a music video for Peter Gabriel, among other projects.

As a film-maker, Julien states that he is 'interested in committing acts of transgression in regard to questions of race and representation,' which means that he's working against narrow ideas of nationalism and identity. Indeed, part of what makes him such a remarkable figure is his engagement with the theoretical debates around culture, politics and representation. He's an important theorist as well as film-maker.

Young Soul Rebels (1991), Julien's latest film, represents a real departure, both for him and for black British cinema. A feature film with a budget of

*Bell Hooks is one of the leading African American feminist theoreticians in the USA.
This interview is reprinted courtesy of *Transition*.

1.2 million pounds, *Young Soul Rebels* centres around two friends, Chris and Caz, who operate a pirate black radio station called *Soul Patrol* in an East End garage. It is 1977, the year of the Queen's Silver Jubilee. The film opens with a murder in the park and ends with a riot at a 'Funk the Jubilee' concert; but in between, it dramatises the richly conflictual cultures of late seventies London. This is a world of punks, skinheads, and young soul boys and girls: of identities in collision, and collusion. Julien and the Sankofa collective stress that they speak from, and not for, the experience of black Britain. But the cultural moment that *Young Soul Rebels* depicts was central to Julien's own coming of age as a youth in London, making it an intensely personal film as well.

This kind of work has a particular fascination for black critics in the United States who seek a way to untie cultural politics with cultural practices, practices that might reach beyond class and national identities. A concern to engage a diverse audience also helps account for the prominent role of the music in *Young Soul Rebels*. More than any other black film-maker, Julien has been concerned with the effects of black American culture on the British experience. If *Young Soul Rebels* has such a 'black American' feel, it's because the music cements a bond between the two experiences.

Julien is not afraid to challenge his audience, but he is not afraid to be popular either. *Young Soul Rebels* – which was chosen to open 'critic's week' at the 1991 Cannes Film Festival [and won the prize! ed.] – displays that distinctive relation to style that has been such an intrinsic part of the diasporic black experience, where elements from high culture and low culture are mixed up into a distinctive funk. Like many other films associated with Britain's black film collectives, *Young Soul Rebels* is both an act of retrieval and an unsentimental exploration of the identities we inhabit today.

BH: The first work of yours that I saw was *This is Not an Aids Advertisement* (1987). Can you tell me a little about what motivated it?

IJ: I was interested in trying to make a more *plural* representation of gay men, and I was trying to make that challenge at a time when we were seeing representational strategies that were closing off a number of debates, whether around interracial relationships, interracial sex – or having sex, period. Because in the current AIDS crisis, it was obviously very difficult to start talking about sexual representations in a different light, with the onslaught of moralistic campaigning that was taking place in Britain especially. There were a lot of anti-sex messages that were being pronounced by the dominant media posters. I wanted to challenge those representations somehow. In a way, that's where the risky business occurs. Looking becomes very important, which is why cinema and image-making become a crucial area in which to try to open up those questions. I think it's very important to have some sort of debate. I mean, I see myself as a kind of political cultural activist: and I see my work as making these kinds of interventions.

BH: When I look at black representation of sexuality in the United States, I often feel like I'm an alien from another planet. There's a kind of flat, one-dimensional texture to the cinematic depiction of black heterosexuality. Which is one reason I was really drawn to your work. And I remember at the first event where I saw *This is Not an Aids Advertisement* and talked to you about it, I asked whether you thought that in your work you eroticize the white body in a way that you don't the black body. And after I saw *Young Soul Rebels*, I have to say the person I really wanted to have sex with was the white male Billibudd (Jason Durr). It strikes me there's a dilemma here: how can we name the black desire of the white body without reinscribing the idea of black self-hatred or distaste for the black body?

IJ: I think in trying to transgress, not on one but on several fronts, be they racial, sexual, psychic or social, there's always this unconcealing of ambivalent 'structures of feeling', to use a Raymond Williams term. And that's why it becomes an exciting new way of uncovering various taboos in black politics or black cultural representations. And one's ambivalence – I think some of Fanon's work point to this – isn't found so much in polemic, in what one says, as in one's fantasies, in one's desires; there's a way in which all these different repressions and oppressions are reinscribed in the psyche. In some of the work I'm trying to to do, I'm trying to propose differences which do make a difference. I think that's the way that one can move forward in some of these debates. Because what's been happening within advertising – and in the commodification of race generally in the Benetton advertisements – is a new racism, encoded in this vision of 'the family of man'.

BH: There's a new ad that has the white male kissing the black woman, but the way he's holding her neck, he could easily be choking her.

IJ: I haven't seen that one, but theirs is the sort of campaign that comes to mind, where difference is articulated in this transgressive way, but for a white audience, I think.

BH: Isn't that a charge that could be made against *This is Not an Aids Advertisement*, if the white male body is marked in the film as the desired body, what with the images of the Greeks and so on?

IJ: In *This is Not an Aids Advertisement*, I think I try to portray a number of different racial bodies; if there was a privileging of the white body, or the Latino or mixed-race body, that had probably more to do with the material that I was working with than with anything else. The truth about *This is Not an Aids Advertisement* is that it incorporates material I shot for some milliner friends of mine, Bernstock and Spiers – a kind of advertisement I was doing. Some of the images I came up with were very interesting, because they're like images one would use in fashion. So what I did was to insert some of this material in the tape I was making, which is why they were constructed in a different way from the other representations of the black male body.

But if I'm honest, I should also admit to a kind of self-policing of myself in relation to black representations of the male body. Because of the historical inscription of male bodies in photography and in art generally, I was always worried about trying not to show the black male body in a particular construction that could be consumed for an unquestioning white gaze. I was worried about that gaze, and that meant that to an extent I annihilated my own ambivalent desire around the black male body. I think that was a problem, and I think that I resolved those things more successfully in *Looking for Langston* (1989), where I really wanted the black male body to be the site of pleasure.

BH: I was really surprised when a lot of people here said the bodies in *Looking for Langston* are too romanticised. Some people saw that film as highlighting the fairer-skinned body, which isn't what I felt.

IJ: I think there's a matter of historical specificity that we tried to preserve: the kind of black men who would have been at the centre of the Bohemian life style would have tended to be black middle-class Americans, and because of certain structures in that society, they were more or less light-skinned. At the same time, it would be kind of crude to say that this representation is privileged, because in representing the Langston Hughes character, and Beauty, I wanted to maintain a degree of faithfulness to the Bruce Nugent poem that I was trying to visualise. Now, in the poem 'Fire', which was published in 1926, the first black gay text to appear in an Afro-American journal, the actual person who was Beauty, I believe, must have been a white man of some kind. Already, in terms of visualising the poem, I had changed that. So there is that kind of argument that I could make, about respecting the specificity of the texts that I'm trying to illustrate in the film visually.

But also I think behind those kinds of accusations there lies something else, which is a kind of closure around racial representations and anything that aims to be slightly ambivalent. For example, when you hear the slogan 'Black men loving black men is the revolutionary act of the 80s', everyone knows we're talking about dark-skinned black men. And again, I sense this closure, this essentialism, in that statement that I feel is problematic, obviously, because I have a white lover. In those terms, is one written off? Is one really black enough? And who is black enough anyway? There are these statements that are being circulated that, to me, point to a rise of nationalism, an essentialism of a different kind.

BH: There's a kind of absolutism in this resurgence of black cultural nationalism, and desire is one of the arenas that it polices. According to the crude nationalism, the decolonized black subject should only have a love object who's black. It's hard for us to formulate paradigms of interracial desire that aren't about the self-hating black man who's looking to the white other for some kind of glorification or betterment; I think in the States, many interracial relations seem still to be rooted in those old paradigms. I think that's one of the issues that *Young Soul Rebels* is trying to address. On the other hand, one of the most powerful scenes for me in *Passion of Remembrance* (1986) is the scene when these two black women, who are lovers, are getting ready to go out, and they're dancing, and they're looking at their bodies. And as a black woman, I felt I had never seen a scene like that in the cinema before, because the black female body was an object for the voyeuristic gaze – there was something about the way that scene is shot that conveys a sense of these black women saying: we're claiming our bodies and our pleasures and our thick lips and our hips and everything.

IJ: For ourselves.

BH: For ourselves. And I know that the scene would have been totally different for me had it been an interracial couple. Identity politics is often a starting point.

IJ: There's been a cultural desert of those representations; you don't have enough black film-makers, including black women film-makers, in a position to make those representations available for a number of different audiences. As a result, you don't have those choices of constructing a particular object. That's where desire in the cinema becomes pretty important for black spectators. But I think one needs this plurality of representational strategies at hand.

BH: I'm in complete agreement with Kobena Mercer's argument, with respect to the absence of black subjects in mainstream film, that sometimes a little essentialism, a little narcissism, is necessary. That's why I say that the image of the two black women is a starting point – but it's not an end point for me. And that's my problem with crude nationalism, where being with a black person is a kind of end point.

IJ: Obviously – because blackness as a sign is never enough. What does that subject do, how does it act, how does it think politically? All of these questions are very much to the point. People will always ask me: what do you think of Spike Lee's films? And my answer would be, well, Spike Lee's films are interesting. But it's not enough: there should be a whole spectrum of black film-makers, including black women film-makers, in a similar position. It's a line I take seriously. But then being black isn't really good enough for me: I want to know what your cultural politics are.

BH: Like Stuart Hall's remark that 'films are not necessarily good because black people make them, they're not necessarily right on by virtue of the fact that they deal with the black experience'. So, for example, *Paris is Burning* – Jenny Livingston's film about black drag queens – has been incredibly celebrated here. I think that many people just see black gay subculture and imagine it's an oppositional film.

IJ: I don't think it's an oppositional film.

BH: But it was interesting to see that, because of its subject matter, people project onto the film a degree of radicalism that is not really there in the film itself.

IJ: To me, one of the problems in *Paris is Burning* is that the subjects in the film are, to an extent, presented to us as objects of a certain gaze which is, in the end, ethnographic. It's a modern ethnographic film set in New York. And why is it that, at the moment, we have a gay culture that is postulating itself in this way? I think it has something to do with the AIDS crisis. And that's something that was never clearly articulated in that film.

BH: It's almost like Mapplethorpe's pictures of black men. Isn't it interesting that the photographers always come just when the tribe is dying out? So too with the 'celebration' in these Mapplethorpe pictures of black men. Better catch them before they die out. One thing that struck me about *Paris is Burning* is that there is no sexuality in the film.

IJ: Desire is not really at play at all in *Paris is Burning*; desire is enacted by the subjects in the film because their fantasies are about being 'Vogue' models or articulating black style in a hybrid way. It has to do with their lack of access to those industries of desire, which channel and create desire and fantasy; real psychic areas for white subjects and from which black people are excluded. Black gay people in particular are parodying all these different styles, and these different representations of fashion – of the cat walk – are very inventive and in some ways very important. People create these houses for different reasons, but I think that the house is attractive because these people realise they need to protect themselves and form their own entertainment when what is presented as entertainment in the US is something that tightly excludes and marginalizes them. All this is rather obvious. But if I made *Paris is Burning*, I'd have to have some kind of critical discourse somewhere that says: where does this leave you? I mean, it's an amazing event, and that's why everybody enjoys the film. Because although there's a realness to that film that we can all relate to, and which in fact we probably all enjoy, there's also this camera with its surveillance-ing quality which is very much present there.

BH: That's why there can be no portrait of desire there. The profound, voyeuristic narcissism of the camera can't pick that up, because it finally isn't interested in desire, in the erotics of this spectacle. Who's interested in how the drag queen fucks, or who the drag queen fucks? The whole emphasis is really on the pageantry and style. But I'd like to go back to the idea of the romanticised and eroticized. I recently saw Marlon Rigg's video *Our Tongues Untied*, and what struck me about it was that a lot of the bodies were positioned in a way that was very militaristic in their pose; there was a posture of hardness, in a way. While Marlon's film language in the film was all about breaking through that representation of hardness, most of the images that we see reproduce that stance. Whereas a lot of black people had difficulty with the eroticism of *Looking for Langston* precisely because the image of the black male body as vulnerable and soft is so antithetical to the way black maleness is represented in this culture, I thought one of the key things in the film was to disrupt the gaze in terms of how it perceives black men; and have this kind of exposure of the realm of desire as also a realm of vulnerability.

IJ: I think that my own project has been one of discussing masculinity, black masculinity in particular, and in a way trying to point out the construction of black masculinity, and by creating gaps, or lacks, in the representations of black men in the films that I make, I try to show a more ambivalent black masculinity, which is something that is masked over. In black popular culture, of course, a black masculinist, hard representation is what's important in articulating polemics against racism and institutionalised racism. But if we're actually trying to create a discussion among ourselves or trying to show another kind of representation, it's important to portray the kind of construction of black masculinity which *is* something that's very fragile and vulnerable.

BH: When I had Oberlin College show *Passion of Remembrance* to all the incoming freshpeople, during the scene where the two black men kissed, a lot of black males in the audience put their heads down. And when I went to the screening of *Young Soul Rebels*, when there were tender scenes of lovemaking and eroticism between black men, I remember Rastas in the audience who were saying 'Stop it, man, stop it!'. That initially registers as a homophobic response, but it's also a response to seeing the public exposure of a certain kind of black male desire that is vulnerable.

IJ: I think it's the kind of transgression which some black audiences are interested in not seeing, not looking at – because within the act of looking, their own insecurities start to unravel. There's also this invitational mode of address which I try to circulate in the images of my films, where they're caught up with the seduction and then it's interrupted, to a certain extent, by these representations. I think that, in a way, it's because of the barrenness of representation in those arenas, in the cinema, that when those representations are up on offer, people do feel exposed. But that kind of unease is important if we're going to progress to learn how to look in a different way; I think that looking in a different way is what's threatening. And this response, this shame, is something that I think holds back important discourse around black male representation in the cinema – and in lived reality. We know that in the black community AIDS is on the increase. And part of the reason for this is repression, and the fixed gendered roles that some black people play into.

BH: It seems that within black life in the States, there is no public discourse of desire. We're still at the stage when we're up against all that nationalist nonsense that birth control, all forms of it, is genocide. Young black men say to the women in their lives, I don't wear a condom because this is a form of genocide. So on the one hand, we're up against that kind of reactionary politics. But on the other hand, how can we talk about the ways that people's desires make it difficult to have safe sex? What would it mean to be able to talk about the desire to feel you possess someone utterly, the desire for certain forms of surrender?

IJ: Well, I think when one talks about desire one obviously has to know that desire is constructed, and one can relearn desire in a different way, in the present AIDS crisis. Because if you don't practice safe sex, then your days of desire may become limited. In general, I think the whole notion of passivity and masochism and all these different notions of transgression in sexual practices were being more fully articulated in blues songs in the 1920s than they are now. And I think that with the advent of this new pseudo-black-nationalism there's a closing off or policing of those different discourses that make it difficult to articulate those desires.

BH: One of my problems with the way Spike Lee as a commodity has functioned in the States is the idea that black film begins with him. If you want to be a successful film-maker – to have millions of people seeing your films in this society – I think it's completely impossible to present the black subject, and certainly the black desiring subject, in any way that radically pushes against convention. Because what so many white viewers are coming to see when they come to see a 'black film' are images that resonate with what they believe to be 'black sexuality'. Think about Spike Lee's appropriation of Eddie Murphy's 'It's a dick thing.' I mean, isn't that absolutely how black sexuality has been constructed in the white colonising imagination – as a completely phallic-focussed sexuality? And Spike does nothing to push against that reading.

IJ: But that is black populist cinema, isn't it? That's what everybody celebrates, and I feel the pressure of people wanting me to do that. In those contexts, it's fine to be phallocentric in those differing kind of black representations, but obviously it's not quite on to have interracial gay relationships.

BH: Think again about the tragic vision of black heterosexuality that's produced in Eddie Murphy's *Harlem Nights*.

IJ: That film was terrible.

BH: Here you have the black man finally getting the black female object of his desire; they get in bed, they make love, and they're plotting to murder one another. And I see this tragic vision echoed in *Mo'Better Blues*, where you come back to the long-suffering black woman who's already been coded in the film as not the object of desire, not the body, but the 'mommy', the tit, the person who's going to make your life work. When you come back with that woman, the only sex you have is the kind that's leading to the reproduction of the male, having the child, and the whole notion of sexual pleasure gets wiped out by the end of the film. We know that a big key aspect of AIDS and a lot of the crisis around black sexuality in this society is either the notion of womanising or having multiple partners; but a lot of that is tied to the notion of the domestic household as the place where sex and desire end, so that one is always moving outside to try to reconnect with some site of pleasure and sexual ecstasy.

IJ: But that could be a problem for white suburban families too, couldn't it?

BH: I think it's even more charged within black life because of the politics of sexuality and space. What happens if you're a large family in a small space? For example, in my family, nudity was just seen as sinful. It was sinful to look at one another naked. So here you had six girls sharing two tiny bedrooms, but we are all desperate not to be seen by the other. What I think is so magical and moving about *Young Soul Rebels* is the degree to which it challenges a lot of these limited, narrow constructions of black sexuality on all fronts. I think it's important that the film does show the black heterosexual man Chris (Valentine Nonyela) as being vulnerable in a way. To me, there's this wonderful moment of the gaze when Chris sees the black woman Tracy (Sophie Okonedo) for the first time and you see that kind of volcanic eruption of desire which the camera catches. And what's powerful about that scene is that it's not the kind of phallic pornographic gaze. There's this whole quality of tenderness.

IJ: For that reason, some people will probably find that *Young Soul Rebels* is not a tough enough film. In that sense it falls slightly short of being, you know, a real 'black film'. Of course, my response would be that I'm trying to create a space for debate around the possibility of different types of representation of black masculinities, heterosexual and homosexual.

BH: Part of the magic of *Young Soul Rebels* is that because it gives us so many diverse black subjectivities, it doesn't run into the issue of: how shall I construct this one monolithic black identity which is 'positive'? It shows that we can have multiple subjectivities at work in the film.

IJ: That was difficult to construct, too. Obviously, while you're trying to construct all this fluidity, there's also the honing down of a narrative structure, and so it becomes quite difficult for those kind of representations to be more than just polemical subjects or political statements.

BH: At times, the character of Chris, the heterosexual man, seemed weak to me. Of course, maybe he seemed weak to me because there was very little about him that defined him as heterosexual in the conventional norms of black masculinity.

IJ: I suppose so, but the thing about the look of Chris in the film is that I wanted to have this sort of ambivalent play-off, with people in the beginning of the film thinking maybe he's gay, but in fact he's a straight character in the film.

BH: But that's the tightrope that the film walks. It problematizes the whole notion that we can look at somebody and read what their sexuality is, that I can see what you do and know that you're gay. One of the ways the film works to challenge this is that, in many ways, Caz (Mo Sesay) has more of the conventional heterosexual characteristics. That's one of the ways the film challenges the looker. It says, you think this is a code of heterosexuality when it's not, or you think it's a code of being gay and it's not.

IJ: Yeah, I think I wanted to play with those representations – but in 1977, young black men did play with those representations, if you think about the whole construction of the young black soul boy, the young black boy who was interested in style and dressing in a particular way which was then considered to be effeminate – wearing buttoned Levi jeans or tight trousers – and which might cost him violence. At the same moment we had punk rock starting to be a strong white youth movement. It was the moment when these different sorts of representations were put up on offer, and this is what I found exciting, that if offered up a different, softer image of black masculinity.

BH: I think, for example, of Prince as personifying that, and it's interesting how critics like Nelson George, even Greg Tate to some extent, have created a kind of suspicion that is cast around figures like Prince and Michael Jackson where their willingness to toy with questions of identity, to toy with construction, gets coded as non-black, as therefore worthy of some kind of punishment in black communities.

IJ: I think it's brilliant what Prince does.

BH: The fact is I don't think Prince pushes himself as far as he could go.

IJ: He probably isn't able to, because there are limitations, the relationship to the music industry and the question of how far you can go before people start to question your identity to a much greater degree. I think the discomfort black critics have with those kind of representations is probably due to their being defensive and to a certain extent essentialist about what black people should look like. And my question is, again: who is black? How black do we have to be for them, whoever they are?

BH: Let me ask whether *you* are going far enough. Part of what was so celebrating for me about *Looking for Langston* and *This is Not an Aids Advertisement* was the feeling that they were pushing against the boundaries. There are going to be people who say *Young Soul Rebels* doesn't push hard enough, it's very Hollywood cinema on some level, it has a straight narrative that can be followed, it has a clear story. Do you feel you had to repress something? There's no visual representations of penises in *Soul Rebels*, for example.

IJ: In Britain, at the moment, I've been having to make the case for *Rebels* to get a fifteen certificate. The British Board of Film Classifications says that to allow fifteen-year-olds and above to see this film, I would have to cut part of the sex scene between Billibudd and Caz.

BH: No !

IJ: If it means that in the end that we have to have an 'eighteen' because we refuse to cut it, then that will be the case.

BH: That's the best sex in the film – we don't want to lose it.

IJ: There is this kind of censorial aspect at work, and I'm working within certain restricted codes. I'm trying to push the limits of those codes. But one of the reasons I was interested in making a more narrative film was that I wanted to address the wider audience. Because at the end of the day, I think you make different films for different audiences.

BH: *Young Soul Rebels* is going to appeal to the audience that sees independent film because it's so transgressive at so many points, but it also has a lot that can draw in a mass audience, including the sound-track, because the music plays a really important role in the film. Tell me what inspired it, because a lot of people are going to say, this is not your Isaac Julien film.

IJ: No, I suppose not. Basically, what inspired me to do *Young Soul Rebels* was the desire to make visible black working-class youth cultures in 1977, when the film takes place. It was a time when there was no expression of black culture in the dominant media anywhere, and so you had a very diasporic relationship to America, in the sense that music was something that was very important – listening to soul records, funk music. As a commodity, it was hard to get hold of: you had to go to specialised record shops to find imports of Roy Ayers or Funkadelic, stuff like that. It wasn't widely available. There were a few people who were into that music, young black – and white – people, and it was like being part of an elite gang of style makers. What was interesting was that it was younger black people who were constructing that style, that 'look', if you like. Of course, punk rock was happening at the same time. I was interested in drawing upon memory, to make use of my own autobiography, and turning it into some kind of historical document. Because listening to Funkadelic, Parliament and all that kind of 'new jazz' if you like – funk jazz – was very important to young black people. And at that time there was just the beginning of pirate radio stations. Not only were no black people being represented in the media, there was no black music being played at all on the radio stations – except for one reggae show and one soul show once a week. What happened, slowly but surely, was that this kind of music became very popular, younger black people wanted to hear more of it. So they started to broadcast illegally and form their own radio stations. And this is part of the narrative of *Young Soul Rebels*. Caz and Chris would probably be among the first younger black people to start playing the music that they wanted to hear.

BH: The sound both carries a sort of nationalistic spirit and invites other people in. You see the same thing in the relation between Tracy and her white friend Jill. We can relish the specificity of blackness even as we can open it up and invite all kinds of people to share in this experience. It's not like the essentialist posture that says: 'We've got our spot of hot blackness over here, and we're not going to let anybody in on it.' The film dramatises a stance of inclusiveness.

IJ: That was an important part of the youth culture emerging in the seventies – you could see it taking place on the dance floor and in the clubs, the simultaneous reproduction of different audiences: gay, straight, black, white. And it was very exciting to have that mixture in the audience.

BH: I'd like to talk about the difference in the budget between *Looking for Langston* and this film, and the departure this represents for you. As it is, when people in the States think about black British film-making, they don't think about collectives, they think about Isaac Julien.

IJ: All that really happened in Britain, in the eighties, is that there's been a whole new wave of black independent film-making. I can see that *Young Soul Rebels* is a departure in some ways. It's the first time that we've had this amount of money granted to us to make a film, and that's because it's a narrative film. We could never get as much money to make an experimental film such as *Looking for Langston* as we got for this one, something like $2.5 million. The whole political, cultural terrain has shifted somewhat, such that it would not be very difficult to try to raise money for a film like *Looking for Langston*. So I think making a narrative film is the kind of strategy that Sankofa is interested in. Maureen Blackwood is also writing a feature film at the moment and the Black Audio film collective is very much involved with narrative in the film that they're working on now, *Who Needs a Heart?*, which is a film about Michael X. They're also interested in shooting on 35mm and receiving more money to do it. But funding institutions are rather wary of giving black film-makers intensive financing.

BH: What made *Young Soul Rebels* different?

IJ: It was a film which was written in a fairly realist way, although when you look at it it's fairly stylised. And I think people were interested in some of the things it was doing, some of the things it was saying. Also, we made the film with the British Film Institute. It was the first film that we made outside of Sankofa. I think because it was a bigger budget film, the funders, like Channel 4, would have felt very nervous about giving all that money to a black film company. So there's a certain amount of politics in trying to develop features. But basically we just pushed very hard. *Young Soul Rebels* was in the developing stages when we were shooting *Looking for Langston*; there was already a fair draft of it. And Colin MacCabe was central in raising some of the finance for the project. He was co-executive producer for the film.

BH: You always talk about 'we'.

IJ: More or less everybody who worked on *Looking for Langston* and *Passion of Remembrance* also worked on *Rebels*. It was the same cinematographer, Nina Kellgren; Nadine Marsh Edwards, a member of Sankofa, was the producer. Obviously, it's directed by me. In that sense, it might be seen as me branching into making my own film.

BH: How do you respond when someone like me says that there's a very Hollywood feel to it.

IJ: In some way I think it's good. I don't believe audiences really want to hear what I'm saying. One has to work within and against the grain of fetishism to draw them to hear questions that they might not want to hear.

BH: That's what I think it does incredibly well. We don't really get that in the States. Amidst Hollywood 'glamour' in your film, there's the dramatisation of desire and murder. And there's the idea of white envy – Ken's envy of blackness and black masculinity – that really hasn't been seen on screen in this way.

IJ: No, and it's something that everybody disavows. A lot of people ask me: why did Ken commit the murder? And I ask myself: why do white men want to hang black men? I mean, is it something to do with Freud's castration complex – or something to do with Fanon's description of white desire and envy toward the black subject, etc. etc.? Ken's not someone who's psychotic; the murder wasn't premeditated.

BH: You get the sense that he's one of the most easy-going regular white boys in the film, and that's why it's so important that he has this envy. He doesn't have the gorgeous style of Billibudd. He's kind of *basic*.

IJ: The thing that's interesting about someone like Ken, or TJ, is that both these two characters have secrets. And what I'm trying to point at is the dangers that circulate around people with secrets. So they both end up in this park at night, but in a way, I'm talking about marginality.

BH: The park scene has this kind of David Lynch quality; it's surreal but it's also hyper-real. I found the silence sequence – where we see TJ up against a tree – to be a highly charged sexual moment. There was a Hitchcock quality, but teetering on the edge.

IJ: It *is* on the edge. In London, recently, there have been quite a number of gay men who have been murdered in parks. There's a debate in the film about the murder, but the consequence of that murder to different communities of interest makes it a debate for all communities. I think that a lot of black men like TJ, who are probably bisexual, who are not gay-identified, go to spaces where they're able to make some sort of acknowledgment of their own desires. I think it's dangerous that people are driven to those spaces. Of course, they may want to go to those spaces, they may enjoy going to them. That's fine. I'm not being moralistic about it. But the character of TJ is meant to be a kind of younger black man who's not 'out' to anybody, and those are the spaces that he goes to. So it's about marginality and the dangers of it. In a different way, Ken, who desires and envies black men in this Fanonian sense, is the opposite side to that. He's someone who can't come to terms with his own desires.

BH: Then how do you characterise Billibudd? Is he someone who overcomes white racism and relinquishes white privilege? Or is he the adventurous white man seeking a thrill? How do you see him as a character?

IJ: Well, Billibudd has some relation to the Melville character, Billy Budd, of course. I see him as someone willing to challenge his white racism; I don't know if he's willing to give up white privilege.

BH: One of the sweetest scenes in the film takes place between him and Caz, when Caz comes over to his place and they turn on the music and you hear this white music, and Billibudd switches it to the black music. But Caz isn't going to have that. It's like: don't put me in this box, I'm not going to be this ethnic thing for you. So instead there's silence. I found it an eloquent statement about the politics of race, even though it was completely non-verbal.

IJ: It's a struggle all the time. Negotiating and re-negotiating, asserting oneself. It's what I was trying to do, but not do it through words. In a way, for me, Billibudd represents the white left. I mean, obviously he's gay, but he's like a socialist, he's got the socialist worker's paper, and he has this romantic idea about making working-class people more socialistic. And, indeed, his relation to black culture is one that is not really examined properly. So I see him as representative of the left in Britain.

BH: To me one of the most marvellous images in the film is the image of Chris and his sister and the other little girls when they're dancing together. There's that beautiful shift that Chris makes when he breaks down and plays with the girls, dances with them.

IJ: His relation with his sisters is one where he's able to reveal a different side of black masculinity.

BH: In diasporic culture, music is so important to us in coming to an awareness of our sexuality.

IJ: It's one of my preoccupations; if you want to look back at this discourse around black sexuality, you have to look at black music. That's really where you see some of the first – and some of the most diverse – articulations of those desires.

Paul Hallam
Derrick Saldaan McClintock
Isaac Julien

Film Script

1 EXT. CITY – Night

City silhouette. Sunset.

Main title: Young Soul Rebels
Soul sounds and punk from 1977: Parliament: P. Funk Wants To Get Funked Up and
X-Ray Spex: Identity.

A DJ Voice-over. He welcomes the listeners to
'Station we funk... the Mother Ship connection... dealers of funky music and P.funk... '
Credits over more of the DJ's upbeat patter:
'Soul Patrol on 107 FM... uncut funk across London town... '

The DJ tells his listeners to
'Come to the Crypt place/ and get some funk in your face...'
before announcing a tune, The Blackbyrds: Rock Creek Park.

Subtitle: London, June 1977 – the Queen's Silver Jubilee.

2 EXT. PARK - Night

A blue-black summer sky. City road sounds in the distance. The quiet is broken by a
radio.

A YOUNG BLACK MAN climbs over the Park fence, moves into the bushes. He
changes station on his radio cassette recorder, tunes into Soul Patrol.

The YOUNG BLACK MAN presses the 'Record' button. The station DJ announces Roy
Ayers: Running Away, a song with an upbeat tempo yet a downbeat lyric:

We don't love each other/like we used to do...
Running away... Running away...
You don't do the things you used to do/
Running away...

The YOUNG BLACK MAN is not alone in the Park. MEN weave slowly through the bushes. Leaves rustle, twigs crack. Shadows and silhouettes.

The YOUNG BLACK MAN rests against a tree.

Matches are struck. The flames come and go like fireflies.

The YOUNG BLACK MAN watches the movements.

Suddenly a white hand strokes the YOUNG BLACK MAN's arm.

The WHITE MAN's voice is unnaturally quiet, edgy. It could be seductive, it could be violent. It has a disguised quality. The WHITE MAN reaches for the cassette player. He tries to turn down the volume.

YOUNG BLACK MAN
    That's a firm hand. What ya want? Don't mess with the sounds, man.
WHITE MAN
    Turn it down mate, draws attention. Don't want an audience.

The YOUNG BLACK MAN holds the cassette player away from the WHITE MAN.

WHITE MAN
    Like it down 'ere, do yer? Come down 'ere regular?

The WHITE MAN snatches again at the cassette player, turns the radio down. The music stops but the 'Record' button is still depressed. The WHITE MAN pulls the YOUNG BLACK MAN towards him in a rough movement.

YOUNG BLACK MAN
    Yeah, but I ain't seen you before. So leggo ma han'...I ain't into no rough stuff, right?

The YOUNG BLACK MAN rests the cassette player on the ground. He kneels, starts to rub at the WHITE MAN's crotch.

WHITE MAN
    Cute, aren't yer?
YOUNG BLACK MAN
    So ya wanna get to know me?
WHITE MAN
    Wot's yer name?
YOUNG BLACK MAN
    Name? You a policeman or what?
WHITE MAN
    Just being friendly, tell us yer name.
YOUNG BLACK MAN
    Man, you're one stubborn white bwoy. OK - Terry. Friends call me T.J.

They kiss, but the WHITE MAN turns violent. He grips T.J. by the neck. There's a brief and angry struggle.

The WHITE MAN's hand grabs at the cassette recorder.

The WHITE MAN runs through the Park.

On the ground - TWO MEN making love, the WHITE MAN stumbles over them...

He drops the cassette recorder.

3 INT. GARAGE – Night

The pirate radio station, hidden round the back of a broken down car.
At the back of the garage.

CHRIS, a nineteen year old light-skinned youth and CAZ, darker skinned and a bit older, are at the turntable. CHRIS's face is reflected in a rotating record.

The minimal lighting reveals little of the room, but the two DJs are clearly dressed soul-style.

The last bars of 'Running Away' play. CHRIS is at the ready. He speaks into a microphone.

CHRIS
And finally from the Players Association: 'I Like It '- out now on the Vanguard label. This is Chris...
CAZ
And this is Caz, coming to you live on...
CHRIS and CAZ
Soul Patrol.
CAZ
East London's most exclusive P. Funk station... reminding you to boogie down Club 7 tomorrow...
CHRIS and CAZ
Eight till late.
CHRIS
See you there.
CAZ
Bye...
CHRIS and CAZ
And may the funk be with you!

CHRIS spins in his chair towards CAZ. They clap hands in air, pleased the session went well.

4 EXT. CAR – Night

CAZ drives to the Park. CHRIS is laid back in passenger seat.

CAZ pulls up sharply.

The car headlamps light up a poster on the Park railings.

A punk-graphic style ad for a 'Fuck the Jubilee' concert.

CAZ

> You going to the concert?

CHRIS

> Oh leave it out. The only music they're into is the 'livin-in-a-Babylon-me-no-have-no-nice-time' music.

CAZ smiles at the exaggerated Jamaican accent.

CHRIS relaxes, takes out a spliff.

CAZ

> FUNK the Jubilee, now dat would be our event!

CHRIS

> That's right. This is for punks an' hippies. So why are we stoppin?

CAZ

> I thought I might get a bit of air...

CHRIS

> Likely story... I'll see myself home then... You are ba... ad!

CHRIS draws on the spliff. Then hands it to CAZ.

5 EXT. PARK – Night

MURDERER'S Point of View (POV)

CHRIS climbs out of the car, CAZ follows.

CHRIS heads off towards the estate.

CAZ walks into the Park. Like TJ before him, he climbs over the fence.

6 INT. BARBERSHOP – Day

A small and intimate barbershop, like someone's front room.

Images of famous black men on the wall – Muhammed Ali, Martin Luther King - a hall of fame mixed in with the usual barbershop postcards and framed certificates.

A MIDDLE-AGED BLACK MAN and TWO BOYS wait their turn.

The BARBER cuts CHRIS's hair.

CAZ is in the background. He flicks through a soul magazine. The cover: Britain's Soul Scene: The Good, The Bad and the Plastic!

CHRIS

> Hey, me can show you how to do a duck's arse.

BARBER

> Look man, I do the best duck's arse in Dalston!

The BOYS fall about laughing at the mention of 'duck's arse'.

CAZ calls across to the BARBER.

CAZ

    Mr Lloyd, can I turn up the juice?

BARBER

    Ah, go on, man.

As CAZ turns up the stereo, the BARBER holds a mirror to show CHRIS the cut at the back.

BARBER

    Have a look...

CHRIS

    Yeah, man, you're not bad at all...

BARBER

    Blessed cheek!

An OLDER BLACK MAN walks into the barbershop. He speaks quietly and soberly so that the BOYS don't hear.

OLDER MAN

    See dem kill a black bwoy in the Park las' night?

MIDDLE-AGED MAN

    What d'you say?

OLDER MAN

    They kill a bwoy in the Park las' night. Man called James, Terry James.

CHRIS turns in the chair, shocked at the news.

CAZ walks out of the barbershop as another MAN enters.

7 EXT. STREET - Day

CAZ walks to his car, he leans on the roof.

He climbs into the driving seat.

He rests his head on the steering wheel.

Rain pours down the windscreen.

CHRIS joins him in the car.

CAZ

    I know it ain't right, but I keep thinking it could've been me, ya know?

CHRIS

    How d'yer know it was roun' that bit of the park?

CAZ

    Why else would T.J. be in the park for fuck's sake?

CHRIS

    I didn't mean it like that, Caz. Christ, I knew 'im as well yer know.

CAZ

    T.J. Chris... T.J....

CHRIS

    Yeah… T.J.… Fuck…

CAZ

    Ain't 'aving it Chris. It ain't real. Not T.J.

CHRIS

    The man says the filth 'ave been swarmin' roun' the estate this mornin' – askin' questions. You didn't see 'im?

CAZ

    Not last night. There was 'ardly anyone there. I thought it was quiet…

8 INT. UNDERGROUND CAR-PARK – Day

CAZ drives into the car-park.

CHRIS climbs out the passenger door.

He walks round to the driver's side. The window is wound down. CAZ stays in the car.

CHRIS

    So yer definitely not gonna come wiv us? It doesn't 'ave to be today…

CAZ

    I ain't stoppin' ya.

CHRIS

    Caz, we've got to get some steady money in, mate. An' I've got to get my Mum off my back. D'yer know what I mean?

CAZ nods.

CAZ

    Just send me yer autograph when ya sign up wiv Metro.

CHRIS

    Look Caz, I can't stop livin' my life coz *he's* dead, can I?

CAZ

    Rest it, Chris. I'll see ya later.

CHRIS

    Where yer going?

CAZ makes some effort to pull himself round.

CAZ

    I'm gonna go down and see Roland 'bout some crisp new tunes. You wait… I'll make tonight so damn funky even the white boys'll shake a leg!

CHRIS

    Some 'ope. An' I thought I was the dreamer.

CAZ

    'Ow d'ya mean?

CHRIS

    Comin' to Metro for employment!

Both smile. CHRIS rests his hand briefly on CAZ's shoulder. He heads off.
CAZ drives towards the Exit.

9 INT. METRO RADIO – Day

An imposing foyer, tall walls, elegant.

CHRIS steels himself to go through.

Working against the elegance of the foyer there is an extraordinary display of Jubilee tat. A vast crown with lights and a fountain dominates the foyer.

And on the staircase that leads off the foyer there's a cardboard cut-out of the Queen, complete with mechanical waving arm.

CHRIS's colour and soul stye stand out at Metro. There's a compensatory cockiness to his step. He passes the SECURITY GUARDS to speak to JILL, the young white receptionist.

CHRIS
　Hi!
JILL
　Hello, can I help you?
CHRIS
　'ope so. I'm 'ere to see Jeff. Jeff Kane, Soul Show.
JILL
　Is he expecting you?
CHRIS
　Yeah, he said to pass by. Me and 'im are good mates.

JILL knows he's blagging. That view is confirmed when JEFF KANE passes through the foyer, acknowledging only herself.

JEFF KANE
　Hello, Jill.

JEFF makes to leave. CHRIS looks at JILL... she nods... CHRIS pursues JEFF.

CHRIS
　Jeff Kane? Hi, Jeff. My name's Chris, Chris Morgan. I'm a big fan of your show, man...I wanted to talk to you about the station's plans...'cos me and my partner Caz, we'd like...

JEFF pats CHRIS's shoulder.

JEFF KANE
　Thanks. Glad you like the show. It's good to meet listeners.

JEFF KANE wanders away. CHRIS catches at him.

CHRIS
　I ain't just a listener... We're DJs... We run a club, we'd like to get more into radio, yer know?
JEFF KANE
　Club DJs, radio DJs... not the same thing. Do you know how many listeners think they'd make DJs? Come on...

JEFF gestures for CHRIS to follow him.

CHRIS

But we're good. Anyway, you still play clubs, don't ya?

JEFF KANE

Less now. A few weeks ago I was booked at some goddam club in Essex. They start giving me this ten-per-cent-black-entry crap, otherwise, they say, their regulars are gonna cause some trouble. I told them to sit on it.

JEFF gestures, CHRIS laughs.

CHRIS

But 'bout us being on the radio...

JEFF KANE

Send in a tape. Make it quality. Try Tony Cortin first, then keep hammering on his door. But I'll tell you something... an hour of soul a week is an hour too much for some. We got these patriotic listeners out there, and they *always* ring.

CHRIS

I thought your show was doing well?

JEFF KANE

It's doing great. That's what they can't handle. But let me ask *you* something...

As JEFF speaks, a young black woman (TRACY) comes down the stairs towards them.

JEFF KANE

... Do you play music for yourself – to party – or for the listeners?

CHRIS

I didn't say at first, but me and my mate Caz, we don't just do a club... we run a station ourselves.

CHRIS takes TRACY in.

JEFF KANE

Okay, okay. You're serious.

TRACY

Tony's screaming for you upstairs.

JEFF KANE

I gotta run. Send in that tape and keep complaining!

JEFF holds up a clenched fist.

JEFF KANE

Be down in twenty minutes if you want to talk some more.

CHRIS

Thanks... Yeah...

CHRIS and TRACY smile at each other. JEFF hurries up the stairs. CHRIS watches as TRACY follows.

10 EXT. PARK – Day

A FORENSICS MAN investigates the scene of the murder. He hands a bag of potential evidence to a POLICEMAN. Police radio sounds in the background.

The area around the scene of the murder has been cordoned off with tape.

CAZ walks into the Park, carrying a Contempo Records carrier bag.

The POLICE continue their work, they dismantle a cloth screen.

Two MIDDLE-AGED BLACK WOMEN walk towards the scene of the murder.

A POLICEMAN lifts the tape to allow the WOMEN to duck under.

They lay wreaths by the tree where T.J. was killed.

The WOMEN cry.

A POLICEMAN eyes CAZ suspiciously. CAZ catches the glance.

11 INT. METRO RADIO – later in the day

TRACY walks down the stairs towards CHRIS.

TRACY
I've seen you before… Maunkberry's.

CHRIS
No, Global Village. Lacy's? Gullivers maybe? Or is it Saturday lunchtime down the 100? I've seen you somewhere, I know it.

TRACY nods.

TRACY
So what are you doing down here, apart from harassing poor Jeff and making Security nervous? Most DJs run a mile when a fan turns up… Jeff's fighting to keep the Soul Show running and along comes you saying you want your own soul show. I think he was pretty polite considering…

CHRIS ducks back, as if fending off the blows.

CHRIS
Okay, cool… I'll split, yeah? Listen, 'ow did you get to work for him anyhow?

TRACY
I don't. I wouldn't mind. I'm on the 'In Town Tonight' show – PA to the producer.

CHRIS
The 'In Town Tonight' show?

CHRIS unfolds a piece of paper from his pocket.

CHRIS
I'll tell you what's in town – where those in the know go – those who tune into Radio Soul Patrol!

TRACY chuckles.

TRACY

Soul Patrol?

CHRIS

107 FM. It's badly funky! I'll leave your name at the door.

TRACY

Oh...

CHRIS has performed the patter and chat-up line, now he makes to go. TRACY calls him back.

TRACY

You'll leave a name at the door?

CHRIS

Yeah, sure!

TRACY

Well, what is it?

CHRIS

Shame!

TRACY

Tracy! Plus one... !

CHRIS smiles. He and TRACY part, CHRIS breezes past the SECURITY GUARDS.

12 EXT. PARK – Day

CHRIS walks across the Park. He keeps to the paths. There is an unease about him. The Park, the scene of the murder, now the site of everyday park pleasures. A JOGGER pounds past CHRIS, startling him.

CHRIS passes a POLICEMAN.

CHRIS finds his nine year old sister, TRISH. She's with two of her FRIENDS. They're some way from where the murder took place. A quick hug for CHRIS from TRISH. She and her friends seem pleased to be talking to a 'big boy'. TRISH jumps to touch the new haircut.

TRISH

Watcha, baldie!

CHRIS

Alright, Trish? What yer doin' round 'ere?

TRISH

Police wouldn't let us play over there. Bloke got killed.

CHRIS

Yeah, I know.

TRISH turns to her FRIENDS.

TRISH

My bruvva's a soul boy, and I'm a soul girl.

TRISH breaks into her soul girl routine. She has obviously practised. She half-hums, half-sings as she dances. They sing and dance to El Coco: 'Let's Get It Together'.

TRISH stops the dance and takes CHRIS to one side.

TRISH

Will yer show us the formation dance?I wanna show my mates, but it's too 'ard. I can't rememba it.

CHRIS

One dance yeah? An' that's it. Mum'll kill me, lettin' you 'ang about 'ere. Ready? One...two...three... four...

The three girls fall into line as CHRIS turns, kicks and steps. Neat, precise movements. The girls are good.

The actual song over the girls' legs as they do a formation soul dance step.

Finally TRISH breaks off, runs to the nearby bushes.

TRISH

Got something to show yer.

She picks up a battered radio cassette recorder, T.J.'s. Left in the murderer's panic.

CHRIS

One... two...three...four...

TRISH holds the cassette player for CHRIS to see.

TRISH

Shame this is broke.

CHRIS looks it over. Unimpressed.

CHRIS

Where d' ya get that?

TRISH

Found it... Can yer sell it for us?

CHRIS

Dunno... it looks *well* broke.

TRISH

Please.

CHRIS

Alright, I'll check it. Come on girls...

They move to leave the Park.

13 EXT. BACKSTREET – Day

CHRIS, carrying the cassette player, is followed by TRISH and the girls. They're still dancing to 'Let's Get It Together'.

CHRIS

Listen Trish, I'll se ya back at the yard. Yer dinner'll be ready...

The GIRLS dance away. CHRIS walks on alone. He passes a National Front slogan, painted on a railway arch wall.

CHRIS bangs his fist hard against the wall.

The MURDERER (seen only from the back) watches as CHRIS ducks under the bridge... walks on...

12 INT. GARAGE – Day

The garage, site of the night-time pirate radio, now seen more fully in the daytime. A large room, a certain grandeur to it. It's almost a shrine to reggae/roots/rasta. Red, green, gold... in clothes, on album covers and posters. There's a boxing punch-bag suspended from the ceiling and a rough and ready shower area.

A battery of homemade speakers, loose wires, valves and a throbbing sound – reggae.

CARLTON, Caz's brother, works on an engine in the middle of the room, his overalls dirty with grease.

As CHRIS enters, DAVIS, a young black man, wraps a small parcel. He pulls out a betting slip to do the job. His customer is a young, white punk, later identified as BILLIBUDD.

BILLIBUDD
Yeah, nice gaff you got 'ere... You got any wiz?

DAVIS
No suh! We don deal in chemicals.

BILLIBUDD watches as CHRIS crosses from CARLTON to DAVIS, touching hands in greeting. CHRIS waits for BILLIBUDD to leave before speaking.

CHRIS
You 'eard about the murder in the Park?

DAVIS kisses his teeth. He clearly doesn't want to talk about it. CHRIS glances at BILLIBUDD.

CHRIS
Look, it's Johnny Rotten...

BILLIBUDD leaves the garage.

CHRIS
Gimme a three pound draw.

DAVIS pulls out a plastic bag full of weed from his jacket, and another betting slip. He sprinkles a cluster of weed onto the slip before folding it up and handing it to CHRIS. CHRIS takes it in one hand, puts it to his nose and smells it. With the other hand he pays over three pound notes.

CARLTON
Go easy on the draw ya know Chris, min' it don' lick aff ye 'ead!

DAVIS takes out the packet of drugs.

DAVIS
Hold on a minute, don' be in no haste.

DAVIS hands the weed to CHRIS and takes the money.

CHRIS

Any sign of Caz?

CARLTON

Only see dat brudda o' mine when 'e wants something...

CHRIS tests the cassette recorder from the park. It seems to be broken. He flips out the tape and crosses to the garage tapedeck.

He takes out the reggae tape, plays the tape from the park.
He's excited to find the tape is of his and Caz's Soul Patrol station.

On the tape: Roy Ayers: 'Running Away'.

CHRIS

You hear that man! Soul Patrol!

DAVIS

Tek aff dat pretty bwoy music, man. Unna Soul bwoy! Ye wanna fling aff dem earring an' tune into the roots man, ye no see?

CHRIS

Bwoy, rest yerself. You're only into the roots 'cos you can't dance!

Everyone laughs.

DAVIS

How you mean?!

The laughter increases as DAVIS turns up the cassette and dances to the music. It's a fast and furious dance, a satire on the Soul Boy style. DAVIS gets wilder in the parody, he's ready to end with a spot spin...

DAVIS

Shuck!

The spin stops halfway...

TWO UNIFORMED POLICEMEN and a CID MAN walk in on them.

The CID MAN switches the cassette player off.

CARLTON

Hey!

CHRIS

Oi, oi... leave the tunes ..

CARLTON

Who ask you for come in here?

They ignore the question. The UNIFORMED POLICEMEN rifle the shelves in the garage, knock things about, upturn boxes, twist aerials and topple spare parts for cars.

CID MAN

Whose premises?

CARLTON

Mine. So what ya sayin?

CID MAN

Terrence James. Friend of yours, wasn't he? He's been murdered.

CARLTON

We heard. So what ya gettin' at?

CID MAN

Anywhere near the Park last night? Dealing were you?

CARLTON

What kind of fuckeries you talkin' about?

CID MAN

Well since he was supposed to be your mate, thought you might have some ideas about it.

DAVIS

Since when you interested in our ideas eh? Eh? But as you say you is –
why don't you go and check your skinhead friends first?

CHRIS (to DAVIS)

True. Since when Babylon cared inna black man murder?

CID MAN

You said it son. Let's go.

The CID Man and the POLICEMEN leave as abruptly as they arrived.

CARLTON punches the punch-bag in anger.

15 INT. CHRIS'S BEDROOM – Day

CAZ is stretched out on Chris's bed. He looks intense, absorbed. He swigs whisky from a bottle.

Jean Carn: 'Don't Let It Go To Your Head' on the stereo.

CHRIS comes in.

CHRIS

Last place I thought I'd find you!

CAZ

Ya Mum let me in.

CHRIS sits down beside him, notices the half-empty bottle, but says nothing about it.

CHRIS

Filth were round the garage. Makin' enquiries an' generally kickin' the place in. An' your bruvva wants us out. Come to think about it, it's not safe now anyway.

CHRIS picks up the Contempo record bag. Tips it up, looks through the records.

CHRIS

Great, yer got them new tunes.

CAZ

Yeah... So what time you on Metro then? Wiv you gone so long, took it they'd given you a programme on the spot.

CHRIS

Look, it was a waste of time, jus' like you said. I spoke to Jeff Kane though... Great, you got the new Slave...

CAZ

Mnnn... mnnn...

CHRIS

Look, I made myself look a right wally. Does that satisfy yer?

CAZ

You actually *met* Jeff Kane?

CHRIS

Yeah, the man 'imself. Hey, is that the new Benson?

CAZ

Yeah, yeah. What'd he say?

CHRIS

He said an hour a week of soul is an hour too much for some - for a starter. Lots of people go and see him, not so many pirates though, Tracy was sayin'...
Donna Summer?!

CAZ

The very latest. I 'ad to fight 'alf the gay disco DJs to get that one. So who is Tracy?

CHRIS selects a record to play. He looks at one of the new ones, it's in a blank, white sleeve.

CHRIS

'Ow come there's nothin' on this label?

CAZ

That's a rejects, ain't it? All the big labels are binning the records now – well, they can't get the black bands on tele, so they can't be bothered to promote 'em.

CHRIS

As if they try though.

CHRIS half-dances to the new record. He still has some of the others in his hand.

CHRIS

... So what else 'ave we? Right, you got the new Parliament, what about the Philly stuff?

CAZ

I can't keep shelling out, can I Chris? We're gonna have to get some advertisin'....

CHRIS

Tried that before. What we need is new listeners, a bigger radius.

CAZ

Yeah, betta aerial, it's the only way. I'll 'ave a word wiv Ken.

CHRIS

Oh yeah? An' 'ow we gonna pay for that?

CAZ rubs his hands together.

CAZ

'Ave to sell my body!

CHRIS

Yeah, I can see you down the Dilly, wiv yer 'Sex' trousers!

16 EXT. ESTATE – Day

A MAN and a WOMAN unfurl a large Union Jack.

They drape it over the railings of a second-floor outside balcony. The beginnings of the estate courtyard's Jubilee decoration.

17 INT. CHRIS'S BEDROOM – Later in the day

CHRIS searches for a cassette. CAZ is seated on the bed absorbed in a 'Black Music' magazine.

CHRIS

> Is that where it is, in the box?

CAZ

> Mnn... yup... yup...

ANN, Chris's mother, a white woman in her thirties, puts her head round the door. She looks to be half-way through getting ready for a night out.

ANN

> 'Lo Caz.

CAZ

> Hello, Ann.

ANN looks to CHRIS.

ANN

> So 'ow did yer get on?

CHRIS

> Forget it, Mum.

ANN

> Well yer went, didn't yer? What did he apply for Caz?

CHRIS

> Look Mum, yer don't exactly apply. Like I said, can you forget it please? It's a joke tryin' there, ain't it Caz?

CAZ refuses to be drawn.

ANN

> Oh yeah, an' it ain't a joke playing at bloody pirates? Chris, when are you gonna bring some respectable money into this house?

CHRIS silently mimics her, it's a speech he's heard before.

ANN

> I'm absolutely sick of it... Anyway, get off yer backside and take Trish round to Caz's Mum's. I don't want her out on her own.

CHRIS

> You out on the town again? Aren't yer gettin a bit past it?

ANN

> You cheeky bastard!

CHRIS

Can't argue wiv that, can I?

ANN grabs CHRIS by the ear.

ANN

You ain't too big for a clip round the ear, you know Chris. You got one of them funny cigarettes for me?

CHRIS

Mums don't smoke weed!

ANN

They smoke it if they pay for it.

ANN smacks the side of CHRIS's head.

ANN

An' if you touch my catalogue money again...

CHRIS

Alright Mum, alright! There yer go.

CHRIS passes her a spliff.

CAZ

I'll run Trish over to Mum's for you.

ANN sits and leans towards CAZ.

ANN

Thanks Caz.... I didn't say anything earlier. Well, what can yer say? I'm sorry about Terry. Friend of yours, wasn't he?

CAZ

Just knew him around. Not close. But thanks anyway Ann. Is Trish ready?

ANN

Yeah. Don' say nuffin to her, will yer? 'Bout the park. She knows somebody's dead, but I think that's all she knows. 'Ow you s'posed to explain it to a kid? Can't even explain the bastards to meself.

CAZ

I know.

ANN

It's only a week since Shuresh's sister got attacked.

TRISH shouts from the hall.

TRISH

Mum, I'm ready.

CAZ

Yeah. Anyhow, gotta go home and get changed. Gotta get sexy for tonight!

CAZ leaves. ANN slaps CHRIS's leg to demand attention. She holds up the spliff for him to light.

18 EXT. REDBRICK ESTATE – early evening.

SPARKY, a white boy, heavily tatooed, wearing full skinhead gear, hangs round the estate. Paint smears on his clothes and a spray can jutting from his pocket.

To get to the car, CAZ and TRISH have to pass him.

SPARKY
> Oi, soulhead, where's yer boyfr... oops, children present, where's yer friend then?

CAZ
> Don't change, do ya Sparky? Always was a little slimebag at school, now you're a bigger one.

SPARKY
> My feelings is really hurt now Caz...

CAZ opens the car door for TRISH to get in. He turns directly to SPARKY.

CAZ
> Yeah, well be thankful it's only yer feelings.

19 INT. CHRIS's FLAT – Evening

Eddie Henderson: 'Say You Will' on the stereo.

CHRIS is stretched out, trying to push himself into a pair of tight, black leather trousers. He tugs the zip. They're at least two sizes too small.

Later: CHRIS has changed his mind... he zips up red leather trousers. He's happier with the effect.

He pulls on tight cowboy boots, but decides against...

20 EXT. ESTATE COURTYARD – Evening

CAZ, in a fresh outfit, returns from dropping TRISH off. SPARKY has been joined by two mates, BIGGS and KELLY. KELLY is a mixed-race skinhead.

As CAZ's car pulls into the courtyard the gang hover round, half-blocking CAZ's way.

BIGGS
> Wot you up to these days, Caz? We 'eard something 'bout some poncy little radio for all yer little soulboys.

As BIGGSY speaks, KEN, a handsome if slightly going-to-seed man, aged about thirty, appears in the shed area, in the background.

CAZ
> Secret list'ner Biggsy? You used to be into it, didn't ya?

BIGGS
> Oi, you wanna watch yerself, soulie. Uvverwise yer might find yerself arrested for one fing or the other..

CAZ notices KEN and moves to speak to him. Away from the gang.

CAZ

You got a minute Ken? Wanted a word... That mixer ya got us.

KEN

Yeah, what about it?

CAZ

It's duff...

KEN

Oh, yer jokin'? Look, tell yer what. I'll come and 'ave a look at it. If I can't fix it I'll find yer something else. Something better this time.

CAZ

Cheap! I ain't linin' yer pockets again, Ken. Specially if ya spending it on shirts like that!... Sad.

CAZ touches KEN's shirt with a gesture of distaste.

CAZ

Nah... forget the mixer. I'm afta a betta aerial, bigger radius. An A.H.?

KEN

I'll see what I can do for yer...

21 INT. CHRIS's FLAT – Night

On the stereo the end of Eddie Henderson: 'Say You Will'. CHRIS dances to the music, he's still getting ready.

CAZ appears at the doorway. Unnoticed he watches CHRIS dance.

CAZ enjoys the sight of CHRIS changing, the successive revealing and concealing of flesh as CHRIS tries to settle on a shirt.

CAZ

You're getting thinner...

CHRIS

Yeah, it's all the 'ard work.

CAZ

I've noticed...

CAZ nods approval at the final selection of shirt.

CHRIS checks out his overall look in the mirror. He's satisfied.

22 EXT. ESTATE BALCONY (overlooking courtyard) – Night

CAZ and CHRIS haul records out onto the balcony. They stop to briefly hug. Part of the building up for the night. They're off...

23 EXT. ESTATE COURTYARD - Night

But as CAZ and CHRIS head for the car, the gang is again in evidence. BIGGSY is perched on Caz's car bonnet.

CHRIS hits BIGGSY with a record case.

CHRIS

Hey, off the metallic...

BIGGSY slides off the bonnet, KELLY plays suggestively with the car aerial.
KELLY

Wanna play wiv yer aerial!

CHRIS hits KELLY with the record case.

KELLY

Oi, watch the cloth, moth!
CHRIS

Piss off!

SPARKY intervenes.

SPARKY

Bit wound up, aren't we? Wot you need is a party, Chris. Comin' to our little Jubilee
get togevver? You could wear your white suit, an' I'll wear mine...

CHRIS speaks in mock East End white...

CHRIS

Thought that was your style Sparky, my son. A big hood to hide yer ugly face, an
slits for yer nasty little eyes.

CHRIS has to push his way to the car, knocking BIGGSY aside.

BIGGS

Oh steady, rocky...

CHRIS joins CAZ in the car.

CHRIS

Give us a lug of that... nice...

CAZ hands a spliff to CHRIS.

24 **INT. CAR – Night**

As CAZ pulls out of the estate, the gang make various obscene, trouser-drop style
gestures.

CAZ reverses sharply to make them jump out of the way. CAZ remains cool
throughout. CAZ puts a tape on the car cassette. The Blackbyrds: 'Time Is Moving
On'.

CHRIS

You don't think they 'ad anything to do wiv the murder?
CAZ

Leave it out, just the usual windin' us up.

CHRIS isn't totally convinced.

CHRIS

    Yer neva can tell wiv Biggsy's lot.

CAZ

    No, but if 'e has had anything to do wiv it, I'll break his fucking neck.

CAZ

    I didn't tell ya, did I? I 'ad a word wiv Ken about the A.H. He's on the case.

They slap hands, back to the mood of anticipation...

25 INT. THE CRYPT – Night

A club in the crypt of a church. The odd tomb and engraved stone plaque remains, and the arches allow for small, disparate groups to appear in, then disappear from view.

It's a young, mixed crowd, 50% black, 50% white. Mixed gay and straight, male and female, punk and soul. Most of the white crowd are punks. The punks stand round the edges like clumps of decaying flowers.

CAZ and CHRIS move towards a raised altar-like platform. Two female PUNK DJs are behind the decks, playing X-Ray Spex: 'Oh Bondage Up Yours', a strong punk dance number:

Punks pogo furiously on the dance-floor.

There is a bit of banter between CHRIS, CAZ and the punk DJs as CAZ sets up a second table, ready to fadeout the X-Ray Spex. CHRIS digs through his record collection. He selects The Players Association: 'I Like It?'

CHRIS

    This is Chris...

CAZ

    And this is Caz.

CHRIS and CAZ

    Soul Patrol.

CHRIS

    You like it, I Like It...

CAZ

    Players Association.

The Players Association: 'I Like It' draws the soul crowd from behind the stone pillars to the dance-floor. Some of the punks move away, others shift into the soul-dancing, an altogether more engaged and stylish dance.

As the record continues, the floor fills. The dancing is close. The unique and extra-ordinary mix of the seventies' soul clubs emerges – girls dance with girls, boys with boys, girls with boys, punk with soul, black with white... A long, held view of the dance.

CHRIS and CAZ touch hands as they see the crowd get down. They're at their closest in creating the club atmosphere. People join in and add to the music - with whistles, tambourines and shouted 'whoop/whoop' sounds.

TRACY and JILL from Metro Radio arrive, unseen by Chris. They stand at the edge of the dancefloor. TRACY looks a little out of place here, her South Molton Street style too upmarket for this crowd. She is a bit older, a bit classier, less street.

JILL might be the right class, but her clothes are markedly high-street. She openly stares at the clubgoers, it's clear she hasn't been to a club like it. JILL and TRACY knock back their fist drinks. JILL, in for a penny attitude, pulls TRACY to the dancefloor.

CHRIS sees the two women making their way through the dancers, finding a space. TRACY edges their dance towards the DJ rostrum. Towards CHRIS. CHRIS goes down to meet them, without saying a word to CAZ.

He dances alone at first, he's a good, vain, self-absorbed dancer. He dances alone till he knows TRACY'S attention is firmly on him. He then breaks the pose and steers himself close...

CAZ watches as the trio of CHRIS, JILL and TRACY forms.

CHRIS looks across to CAZ at the deck, breaks from the dance. TRACY continues to dance with JILL, but watches as CHRIS rejoins CAZ at the deck. CAZ and TRACY exchange looks.

JILL is distracted by styles and colours, ears pierced with multiple ear-rings, 'granny shoes', tight jeans, baggy trousers tightened at the ankles, plastic sandals, cowboy boots, pointed shoes, collarless shirts, ripped fish-net stockings, jackets made out of plastic bags, maxi-skirts, mini-skirts... and that's just the soul crowd! A PUNK then catches her attention, he wears a pair of Union Jack briefs tacked to his jacket. He notices as she laughs.

TRACY tries to smile at CHRIS, but CAZ is in the way, and when he's with CAZ, CHRIS seems to be avoiding her.

A BLACK BOY, his hair dyed blond, wearing a very thick, purple mohair jumper, dances up to TRACY. She accepts the unspoken invitation to dance. Though the dance involves holding hands, there is a distance between them. JILL jumps around with THE UNDERPANT PUNK, sending him and his dance style up...

The pattern on the dancefloor changes. People form two circles. In the first – two black boys and a white boy. In the second – a black boy and black girl. We lose sight of JILL and TRACY. CHRIS and CAZ sort through their records, CHRIS keeps an eye open for TRACY. It's a while before he speaks.

CHRIS
    Did ya see that girl?
CAZ
    What girl?
CHRIS
    The one I was dancin' with. Tracy.
CAZ
    Oh.
CHRIS
    She's the one I was tellin' ya about... works at Metro.

CAZ

She's well out of your league. What ya ask her down 'ere for?

CHRIS

Do I object to your friends comin' down 'ere?

CAZ

Na. Nice to be liberated, ain't it?

CHRIS

Look Caz, I didn't mean it like that. Hey... What ya sayin'?

CAZ

Rum and coke, large!

CAZ fades out The Players Association, fades in: Funkadelic: 'One Nation Under A Groove'.

CHRIS leaves CAZ at the turntable. CHRIS pushes through the dancers, disappointed not to see TRACY. Quite close to the DJ platform there's a small group of PUNKS. BILLIBUDD, the punk who tried to score at the garage, is one of them.

BILLI has his eyes fixed on CAZ. CAZ notices the cruisy stare and smiles.

CHRIS sees JILL and the PUNK, he laughs as she interrogates the soft-spoken, middle-class, art-school boy. JILL knocks back the drink. She nods at CHRIS but her attention is on the two men behind him – the men are kissing.

CHRIS finds TRACY. She's talking to the PUNK DJs. He hovers, waiting for a chance to speak to her alone. KEN, the equipment dealer, bumps into CHRIS. KEN looks out of place in the club, he's more an East End pub disco type. He manages to slop beer onto CHRIS's shirt in the crush near the makeshift bar.

CHRIS

Shit, Ken! Watch it wiv the drink...

TRACY notices the drink incident.

KEN

Sorry... Sorry... Thought I'd come and check the club... spoke to Caz 'bout the aerial today... I'm working on it. Look, let me get you a drink...

CHRIS

No. No, Ken... No...

KEN

What, yer busy ?

CHRIS

Yeah... Yeah...

CHRIS is clearly annoyed about the shirt, and he wants to be on his own with TRACY. KEN gets the message and leaves.

CHRIS turns to face TRACY.

CHRIS

I'm getting 'em in, Tracy. Do you want a drink?

TRACY holds up her full glass.

TRACY

I've got one thanks... It's a bit mad in here, nice though!

CHRIS

Yeah, listen Tracy, gimme a shout before you leave, yeah?

TRACY

You're not going to join us?

CHRIS

I'm gettin' one in for Caz. I'll see you afta, yeah?

CHRIS smiles and leaves, pushing through to the bar. Everybody knows him. He turns down the gestured 'let's dance' from two guys doing the bump at the edge of the dancefloor.

DISSOLVE: To much later in the evening.

JILL and TRACY are well plastered. JILL tries to avoid the now rather pressing attentions of the PUNK.

JILL

Stop it...

She steers TRACY into a quiet corridor, away from the dancefloor.

TRACY

What are you like?... So what do you think of the Crypt then Jill?

JILL

It's good. I've never been to a coloured... a black club before. Not to mention one wiv blokes kissin' in it.

TRACY

It's only fashion, Jill...

JILL

Nah?

TRACY

I'm only kidding... !

JILL laughs.

JILL

You know what Trace, when you first started at Metro I thought you was a bit of a snob... but we've 'ad a good laugh, ain't we?

CHRIS, seeking TRACY out, interrupts.

CHRIS

Tracy, Tracy..... So what you hidin' from, eh?

JILL

A punk in red, white and blue underpants!

CHRIS

My God, you 'ad his trousers off?

JILL

No! They was on the back of his jacket!

They move back towards the dancefloor, laughing. But CHRIS clearly wants to talk to

TRACY, JILL is a bit in the way. She registers the fact.

JILL

> God, I can see when I'm not wanted.

A PUNK places his arm round JILL's neck.

PUNK

> Oi, get dancing!

They move into the dance.

Later: CHRIS and TRACY in mid-conversation.

TRACY

> ... I don't know... I want to extend it to clubs. What's *really* happening. They've got
> no idea at Metro. The programme is dead.

CHRIS

> Yeah... so what you suggestin' then?

TRACY

> I'm suggesting that you make up a tape, and leave the introductions to me.

CHRIS

> Are you serious?

TRACY

> I'm sick of being a PA I want to make some changes Chris. Are you interested?

CHRIS

> Yeah, you bet!

CUT TO:

**later in the evening. CHRIS at the decks. JILL and TRACY dancing together, JILL
getting a bit out of order, enjoying herself hugely.**

**CAZ is by the bar. He talks to IRVINE, a young black man. IRVINE is dressed in red,
skin-tight jeans with see-through plastic pockets and a bright green top. In spite of
being very much dressed for the club, he's visibly low.**

As they talk KEN passes by. CAZ ignores him.

CAZ

> It's jus' the thought of T.J. lyin' there... That boy could really dance...

IRVINE

> Don't think about it, girl, don't do no good!

**CAZ laughs at the 'girl'. He looks over to a fairly quiet dancefloor, then up to CHRIS.
CHRIS catches the look.**

**CUT TO: CHRIS changing the record to the fast and funky sound of War: 'Me and My
Baby Brother'.**

**A line of dancers, predominantly black, forms. They bump with shoulders, hands, hips,
groins - the speakers tremble.**

**CAZ and IRVINE join the dance. They give the dance everything they've got... an
undefeated, controlled yet wild dance.**

26 EXT. GRAVEYARD/STREET BY CLUB – Night

CAZ and CHRIS carry record cases through the churchyard to the nearby sidestreet. They pass TWO PUNK WOMEN kissing. Jill's UNDERPANT PUNK sits looking startling and miserable on a tombstone. Most of the club crowd have gone. They're still half-dancing as they pack up for the night.

CHRIS
Now that was... Soul Patrol... Soul Patrol ...
CAZ
That was a cool night.
CHRIS
Yeah... Listen Caz, I wanna make a tape up, somebody asked me.
CAZ
So what you up to now Chris?
CHRIS
Nothin'... Jus' need a few of the records. Some of the imports. I'll get the last lot...

CHRIS goes back to fetch the rest of the records. CAZ knows he's up to something, and he's annoyed about it.

A COUPLE of MEN stagger up to the car.

MAN 1
Where'd yer get the motor, man?
MAN 2
Look at that car, man!

CAZ jumps in the car and drives off.

CHRIS is stranded with four boxes of records.

CHRIS
Caz! Where are you? Shit!

TRACY is parked across the road, she laughs at his burst of temper. CHRIS steps to the car, leans in at the open window.

TRACY
What's with your friend?... Need a lift?
CHRIS
Caz has got the 'ump. Can I put the records in the boot?
TRACY
Sure.
CHRIS
Thanks... Nice car...
TRACY
Thanks.

TRACY gets out, opens the boot. CHRIS puts the records in.

CHRIS
So where's yer mate, Jill?

TRACY
> Doing it with that punk!

CHRIS
> Nah!

TRACY
> Yeah!

They lean against the boot.

TRACY
> So where to ?

CHRIS
> Tracy... Can I trust yer?

TRACY
> What do you mean?

CHRIS
> Tell you in the car...

CHRIS gets in the passenger seat. TRACY drives...

27 INT. GARAGE – NIGHT

Torchlight. Searching the cluttered shelves. The light rests on TJ's cassette player – where CHRIS left it.

The gloved hand of the intruder grabs the cassette player.

28 EXT. STREETS – Night

CAZ drives. On the car cassette: Dr Buzzard: 'I'll Play the Fool'. A crossover song, a mix of soul and disco, with elements of the big band dance sound.
> meet a guy/ain't it funny.../
> keep on dancing... keep on dancing...

He halts at a set of traffic lights. In the car alongside, BILLIBUDD - the punk from the garage and the club. CAZ and BILLIBUDD exchange glances.

The lights change. BILLI changes lane, pulls ahead...

CAZ's car eventually following BILLIBUDD's.

29 EXT. EDGE of PARK – Night

BILLIBUDD locks the door on his car, he looks round to see if he has been followed.

He climbs the fence, moves into the Park.

CAZ drives to the edge of the Park, pulls up behind BILLIBUDD's car.

30 INT. GARAGE – Night

TRACY and CHRIS stumble through the garage in the dark. They're laughing, a bit drunk.

TRACY
Well, there's not much to it, is there? Through here?

CHRIS
Yeah, yeah...

TRACY
God, it reminds me...I used to listen to Caroline a lot... I even remember Radio 390, the R & B show.

CHRIS
That dates you.

TRACY
Shut up!

TRACY knocks the punch-bag at CHRIS.

CHRIS
Missed!

CHRIS leads her through the broken down car, into the hidden pirate radio base.

TRACY
Fancy having a radio station at the back of a garage.

Once they're through to the base, CHRIS seems awkward.

CHRIS
Tracy, er... would you like to... are you going to... you could stay you know and... save me...

TRACY
What, here? No chance! You're joking...

They kiss. CHRIS is all for going further.

TRACY
Hey, I've got work in the morning. And you're gonna make me a tape, remember?

CHRIS
Yeah... Right... Yeah...

31 EXT. EDGE OF PARK – Night

CAZ listens, there is a man following him.

CAZ is near the murder spot. There is little light. The footsteps are unnerving.

Something of the tension of the opening scene...

But it is BILLIBUDD who follows him.

They turn to face each other.

BILLIBUDD untucks CAZ's top.

CAZ

You pick your places, don't ya? You heard what happened?

BILLIBUDD

I heard.

CAZ

Ya like living dangerously?

BILLIBUDD

I just wanna show the bastards – I ain't stoppin' comin' 'ere. Brought this with me. Get them in the eyes if there's any trouble.

BILLIBUDD brings out a small anti-perspirant spray can.

CAZ laughs.

CAZ

Any good trouble and ya'll smell nice afta!

BILLI laughs. He presses the spray, in play.

BILLIBUDD moves to kiss CAZ. To get into his trousers.

CAZ is still on edge.

CAZ

Not now, not now. Not here... it feels a bit weird. Give us yer number.

BILLIBUDD

Yeah, yeah... I've heard that before.

CAZ

Nah, it feels a bit weird... Give us your number... I mean it.... I mean it...

BILLI takes out a felt tip, he lifts up his t-shirt....

BILLIBUDD

Your number. Write it here!

CAZ writes his number across Billi's bare chest... .

32 EXT. STREET – Night

The back of a MAN in a telephone booth.

The MAN disguises his voice, muffles it.

MAN

Listen... I was there... he mugged him. His name's Chris Morgan. I think he lives on the Ladywell...No – I can't give my... no names... right?... No... no.

The MAN slams the phone down.

At the MAN's feet - T.J.'s radio/cassette recorder.

He picks it up, leaves the booth.

33 INT. GARAGE – Night

CHRIS runs the tap of a makeshift shower. He sticks his head under it. He notices the big beer stain on his shirt. He takes the shirt off, tries to get the stain out with soap. It won't go.

He curses and returns to the deck. He works fast, by lamplight, to compile a tape. He links the songs with a DJ's patter. He listens to part of the tape, already finished.

CHRIS

Uncut funk at he bop... coming to you directly from the Mother Ship... on top of the chocolate Milky Way... five hundred thousand kilowatts of P Funk.

He speaks into the microphone.

CHRIS

This one's dedicated to all you East London funketeers out there, Parliament... P. Funk... we funk, you've got the funk...

Parliament: 'P. Funk Wants To Get Funked Up' plays.

CUT TO: CHRIS reaches for a fag, but he's out. He seems stuck for an idea. Finally he remembers the tape his sister gave him. He looks across to where he left the cassette recorder. He notices it has been moved, he's not unduly concerned.

He took the tape out, he has it. He plays the park tape, lets it run beyond the song: 'Running Away'.

Suddenly the WHITE MAN (MURDERER's VOICE) can be heard, albeit a bit muffled and crackly.

WHITE MAN

Like it down 'ere, do yer? Come down 'ere regular?

T.J.

Yeah, but I ain't seen you before. So leggo ma han'... I ain't into no rough stuff, right?

34 EXT. ESTATE - Shed/Dustbin area – Night

T.J.'s radio cassette player burning, melting on a pile of rubbish.

35 INT. GARAGE – Night

CHRIS, exhausted, lies back on a car seat.

He runs his hands over his chest, over the crotch of his jeans.

There's someone watching, unnoticed. We see CHRIS touching himself from an unidentified POV

36 EXT. GARAGE FORECOURT – Early morning

A milk lorry passes the garage.

37 INT. GARAGE – Early Morning

A MAN'S gloved hand. A tense, stealthy movement of the MAN through the garage....

CHRIS's feet protrude from the backseat of the winched up car. He's fast asleep.

The MAN's head is covered with a metal mask.

The gloved hand grabs at Chris's feet, making him jump... But the hand is DAVIS's – the gloves, work gloves. The mask – for car repair/welding.

DAVIS
Yo!
CHRIS
What.... Jes.... Davis....
DAVIS
Yow! Check dis brudda boot nuh!

DAVIS has arrived for work, CARLTON follows him in. CARLTON stares at CHRIS'S footwear.

CARLTON
Waht we 'ave here?.... Daggers? Hey bwoy, min' you don' kick me wi yo daggers, ye hear?

CHRIS is not in the mood, he looks at his watch.

CHRIS
Oh no... Sh...it!

He runs out past the bemused CARLTON and DAVIS.

38 EXT. TUBE STATION – Morning

At the tube CHRIS has to push past FIVE POLITICOS. A youth has his back to CHRIS, his leather jacket bears a painted 'Anarchy in the UK' slogan.

The youth turns round, his front lapel is covered in badges... like a noticeboard for the left of 1977. It's BILLIBUDD.

CHRIS half-recognises him from the garage. He catches hold of BILLIBUDD'S lapel, peers at the badges: various distorted images of the Royal Family, Mary Whitehouse with 'Gay News Fights On' across her features, Punk badges, Grunwick support, Stuff the Jubilee... But CHRIS takes issue with one badge in particular.

CHRIS
So disco sucks, does it?
BILLIBUDD
Mindless, capitalist crap!
CHRIS
And punk's not?
BILLIBUDD
Depends how you use it. Don't it?

He hands CHRIS a 'Fuck the Jubilee' concert flyer. A list of bands.

BILLIBUDD

Should be something there you could dance to...

BILLIBUDD is provoking/flirting, looking CHRIS over.

CHRIS

Jumpin' up and down like my arse is on fire.

BILLIBUDD

No, no, no... We've got reggae bands billed. Look, Misty and Roots, you'd like that, wouldn'd yer?

CHRIS (sarcastic)

Oh Wow! Look... I'm in a rush...

AN ASIAN PUNK GIRL interrupts.

ASIAN PUNK

Ain't there more important things to talk about fo' fuck's sake. Like this for instance.

She starts to read from a leaflet, a list of recent racist attacks in the area.

ASIAN PUNK

Like two Somalis burnt to death, arson. Like flats doors kicked in, windows broke. Like Bengali schoolkids getting their faces kicked in. Join a picket 'bout police indifference?

She hands CHRIS the roneod leaflet. CHRIS looks it over, it is a long and horrific catalogue of attacks. CHRIS takes a few copies.

CHRIS

Alright, alright. Look, I'll place a few of these. Did you hear about that murder in the Park?

ASIAN PUNK

Yeah, same night I was running these off.

CHRIS heads down the tube steps. BILLI is still watching him. The ASIAN PUNK GIRL turns to BILLI.

ASIAN PUNK

Cock on the brain you 'ave.

39 INT. METRO RADIO/RECEPTION – Later in the day

CHRIS talks to JILL at reception.

CHRIS

D'yer get his pants off then?

JILL

I can't remember...

CHRIS looks at his watch. He's restless, impatient.

He looks relieved when TRACY arrives.

TRACY

Ready for the verdict?

CHRIS

It's pretty obvious, ain't it? I mean the tape wasn't exactly professional...

TRACY

Stop worrying Chris. I told him you made the tape up last night. It's only an impression he's after. I think I'm getting somewhere with this club idea... And, er... can you keep quiet about your pirate credentials? He's dead set against that.

CHRIS

So who's supposed to play our music then?

TRACY

You don't have to tell me. Come on, we'll be late.

They leave Reception.

40 INT. CITY RADIO STUDIO – Day

CHRIS and TRACY walk into a studio to find DAVE, a white, middle-aged, middle-class producer, listening to Chris's voice on tape.

TRACY

Hi Dave, this is Chris Morgan.

As DAVE talks he walks around and leans on his desk.

DAVE

Take a pew Chris. Yes, well, nice choice of music, if a bit obscure. But you come over well. It's just that it's a bit, um – how shall I say, er – casual. I mean not everybody will understand what you're trying to convey. I like it, but the powers that be... Listen, Chris - to be honest with you – if we were to take you on as a presenter – out and about in the clubs... if we were – and that's a big if – we'd be looking for a more recognisable style, something a bit more... um..

CHRIS

English?

DAVE

Yes... well...I wouldn't put it quite like that... but... er...

CHRIS performs a DJ act, imaginary microphone in hand.

CHRIS

'Ow 'bout this...... 'bout nah, bringin the man cal' Jah Fatman singin: Ye can' keep we down cause we all aroun'... Step forward yout', come let me tell de trut'... That do yer?

DAVE

There's clearly no point in our continuing. I was merely offering professional advice, but it's obvious you're not interested. Tracy, I've got a programme to do. I'll speak to you later...

DAVE leaves.

TRACY

You stupid arrogant fuck! I went out of my way to get you in here. Bang goes my idea.

CHRIS

Shame, innit? The man missed his chance of signin' up a mega-star.

TRACY

I just can't believe this punk, 'no-future' attitude.

CHRIS

I ain't no punk. What are yer suggestin' exactly? Was I supposed to play Elvis Presley records and sound like Tony Blackburn? They've gotta realise that I am your original, your wicked... Pee-funk-a-del-ic- wanna-get-people-all-funked-up-DJ.

TRACY

You've got no idea.... come on...

TRACY catches CHRIS by the arm and leads him to the door...

41   INT. METRO RADIO/OFFICE – Day

TRACY leads CHRIS into a cramped office, picks up a cardboard box and places it on the desk.

TRACY

Jeff Kane, one of the best. Right?... See this?

TRACY looks into the cardoard box.

TRACY

His office! This is what he gets for his five years and the sacks full of fan mail. He's the only black D.J. in the whole place, and still he's offered a contract he has to renew every three months.

TRACY looks round the cramped room.

TRACY

This is where they'd like to keep him, keep all of us for that matter.

CHRIS

Why'd yer stay if they insult you all the time?

TRACY

They're not gonna run me out that easy.

CUT TO:

42   INT. CITY RADIO RECEPTION AREA – Day

The cut-out QUEEN waves.

CHRIS walks quickly down the steps that lead into Reception. He gives the Queen's waving arm a sharp chop.

He lunges into the Jubilee crown/fountain.

Panics the SECURITY GUARDS. But he's out the door before they can catch him.

The cut-out Queen still waves, but more limply now.

43 EXT. PARK – Day

CHRIS, hot and restless, wanders the park.

Finally he settles by the pond. Near a YOUNG FAMILY.

Radio sounds over: A DJ tells the story of the Sex Pistols' recording of 'God Save the Queen', the initial pressing of a thousand copies. A & M's disassociating themselves from the group and the record.

A WOMAN re-tunes her radio.

CHRIS lays back on the grass, to rest and think things over...

Later: CHRIS still stretched out on the grass. TWO SUNBATHING WOMEN to the side of him.

A man stands menacingly over CHRIS. He looks down on CHRIS's vulnerable, sleeping form.

CHRIS's eyes open, startled. He looks first at the man, now recognisable as the plain-clothed CID MAN, then at the back-up: TWO POLICEMEN.

CID MAN
    Alright, son?

The CID MAN addresses one of the POLICEMEN.
CID MAN

    Okay...

The POLICEMEN converge on CHRIS, pull him to his feet.

CHRIS
    What yer doing....?

They're dragging him off.

44 EXT. POLICE STATION/ENTRANCE – Day

KELLY, the mixed-race skinhead from the estate is let out of the station as CHRIS is led in. KELLY smirks at CHRIS. CHRIS is confused. A POLICEMAN hurries CHRIS into the station.

POLICEMAN
    Come on...

The CID Man follows them into the station.

45 INT. POLICE STATION/INTERVIEW ROOM – Day

Close on CHRIS's socks.

Part-way into an interrogation. CHRIS is facing the CID MAN over a table. Both are seated. The PARK POLICEMAN takes notes. The CID MAN ducks his head down to look at Chris's feet.

CID MAN

What sort of socks are those?

CHRIS

What?

CID MAN

I said... What sort of socks are those?

CHRIS

What's that got to do with anything?

PARK POLICEMAN

The man wants to know about your socks.

CHRIS bends down, udoes his shoes, pulls of a loud flourescent sock and drops it slowly onto the table.

CID MAN

Listen smartarse, no monkey business. You don't seem to realise, do you? You're not in here for showing disrespect to Her Majesty at Metropolitan Radio. No, nor for running your jungle bunny club on hallowed grounds, neither.

CHRIS

So what yer tellin' me?

C.I.D. MAN

We know all about yer, that's what. We've been watching you.

CHRIS is increasingly uneasy.

CID MAN

Oh and you might be interested to know we've heard of your tinpot little radio station...

This knowledge seems to worry CHRIS more than anything so far.

CHRIS

I'm not sayin' anything. I'm entitled to a phone call, right?

CID MAN

You can tell Mum all the news later. But it's not the radio. And you're not here for snatchin' some poor dear's handbag. You're in here for murder.

CHRIS is shocked almost to the point of nervous laughter.

INTERCUT WITH:

46 EXT. GARAGE FORECOURT – Day

CARLTON works on the car he worked on before.

DAVIS does business with KEN. KEN is considering a car, a price sticker is splashed across its windscreen.

CAZ polishes the car that interests Ken. CARLTON shouts out to CAZ.

CARLTON

Yo! Sweetbwoy! Come over 'ere and 'elp me wiv dis dam engine. I'm tired an' the man comin for it tonight.

CAZ

Ye mad? I ain't going near dat engine. You mus' want me to nasty up ma garments.

DAVIS

Dam pretty bwoy no wanna help nobody. If he can drive the motors he should be prepared to dirty up him clothes too. Man going like a African prince - or should I say princess?

CAZ

Piss off, Davis.

KEN runs his hand on the bonnet of the car.

KEN

Can I take her out for a spin, then talk prices?

DAVIS

Yeah, Ken. No problem.

KEN approaches CAZ.

KEN

What d'yer reckon then? Is it worth it?

CAZ

Well, there's nuffin' wrong wiv it.

KEN

You 'ave a word wiv Davis 'bout the price an' I'll 'elp you out with that gimmick you're after.

CAZ

Betta be worth my while, Ken.

KEN climbs into the car. Drives off...

DAVIS

Easy now, Ken. She fast.

DAVIS boasts to CAZ.

DAVIS

Take notice soulhead... Number One salesman roun' dese parts!

CARLTON catches the conversation.

CARLTON

Why, ye sell it?

DAVIS

Good as done. Ye no see me 'av the deadly patter? Deadly! Yeah bwoy...

47 INT. POLICE INTERVIEW ROOM – Day

CHRIS has lost much of his earlier spark. The questioning is wearing him down.

CID MAN

Are you gonna tell us? Where were you the night before last?

CHRIS

Easy... . I was wiv me mate, makin' up tapes.

Look, I want my phone call...

CID MAN

Not impressed. 'Wiv me mate'. And do you think that'll hold? Suppose I tell you that you were seen, you and your mate, by the Park that night? Drives a Triumph, right?

This catches CHRIS off-guard. If he tells them he and CAZ were broadcasting, then it gives the pirate away. Now he has to lie.

CHRIS

So what? It's the truth I'm telling ya. I want my phone call. You ain't got nothing on me.

The CID MAN opens a cupboard. He takes the badly burnt cassette recorder out of a plastic bag. He holds it (in gloved hands) to CHRIS's face.

CID MAN

Seen it before?

CHRIS is now totally unnerved, he has handled the recorder, but if he says he has...

CHRIS

No.

CID MAN

No? Your kid sister has. She was seen with it in the Park, before you burnt it, that is. Panicked did you? Tried to burn your dirty black paw marks off it, did you?

CHRIS looks across to the PARK POLICEMAN, furious at what appears to be a set-up, and furious that Trish has been involved. He shouts out.

CHRIS

You bastards. Bastards! What ya doin' gettin' at a nine year old kid?

CID MAN

You're calling me a bastard. You'd kill to get your filthy muggin' hands on a bit of plastic. Kill one of your own. I say one of your own, not that you'd see it that way – you being a half-breed, a mongrel...

CHRIS can't take it. He screams out.

CHRIS

I want my phone call, my phone call, my phone call!

CHRIS thumps on the table... repeats his demand over and over... his movements restrained by a POLICEMAN.

CID MAN

Went back to find it, didn't you? Whatever your little sister says. She stuck up for you, so just who is involving kids in this? Give the coon his call...

The CID MAN lights a cigarette, and casually leaves.

A POLICEMAN places the phone in front of CHRIS and leaves.

CHRIS is left on his own.

He picks up the phone, tries a number, mutters 'Caz, Caz' into the receiver. Panic in

his voice. There is no reply. He slams down the receiver. Picks it up again and dials.

He half-sings a Metro Radio jingle, to jog his memory. The jingle incorporates the station's number. He dials the number.

CHRIS

Hello... can I speak to Tracy... no...no...no I don't know her surname... she works on the 'In Town Tonight' show. Look, *look*, it's urgent, please... Just use the fuckin' tannoy!

There is a pause as he waits.

48 INT. GARAGE - DAY

CARLTON is in the garage's rough and ready shower. Scrubbing off the oil and grease. Slow movements, he's proud of/enjoys his body.

KEN is back from the test drive. Watching CARLTON, but talking business with DAVIS.

KEN

Yeah, Davis. Like the motor. Just a question of the right price.

CAZ throws the car's keys to DAVIS.

KEN puts his arm round CAZ and walks him away from CARLTON and DAVIS.

KEN

Did you 'ave a word? I got you that present. Should do yer nicely.

CAZ

Believe it when I see it, alright Ken?

KEN

Trustin', aren't yer?

CAZ continues polishing the car. KEN leaves.

DAVIS calls across to CARLTON.

DAVIS

Hey Carlton, dem say they're lookin' for a half-caste bwoy now for that murder...

KEN's POV: CARLTON emerges from the shower, drying himself. Kissing his teeth.

CARLTON

Can't trust dem 'alf caste bwoy ye no. Ye don't know which side them on. I could well believe it was one a dem kill that black bwoy.

DAVIS

No, man. Dat's what they wan' you to think. So when the people dem say 'What you gonna do 'bout the murders?' Babylon can say, 'Is black a kill black'. I don' see it.

CARLTON

Well, as far as I and I concern, musa be a white bwoy, an' if it wasn't a white bwoy, I'll lay on money it was a 'alf caste.

KEN is back, listening in.

KEN

    Nah, I reckon it's an NF job myself... See yer later.

KEN leaves.

CAZ

    Are you serious? Ya tryin to wind me up again?... Yeah, it's true it most probably was a white bwoy kill T.J. But it could have been a black man. So what ya sayin? It can't happen? What exactly you gettin' at Carlton, with all this 'half-caste' crap?

CARLTON

    Caz, the trouble with you, right – can't always tell what side you're on.

CAZ

    Now what ya sayin'? What, 'cos Chris is my mate? Or 'cos I mix with white peop...

DAVIS

    MAN! White MAN!... Nastiness!

CAZ

    So dat's wot it's about, yeah? I mix with white man... I *fuck* with white men!

DAVIS

    Jesus!

CAZ & DAVIS are near to blows. CARLTON intervenes, steering CAZ away.

CARLTON

    Long as *you* doin' it to *them*... innit Caz?

DAVIS

    Min' the rod a correction no fuck up dem...

CAZ turns on DAVIS.

CAZ

    You're fulla shit Davis! The bruvva dat got killed on the park – he was what you call an anti-man, a bwatty bwoy. Dat make it alright now? You concerned 'bout who did it now?

DAVIS hesitates, he has no quick answer.

CAZ throws down his cloth, leaves the garage, not waiting for one.

49 **EXT. STREET – Afternoon.**

TRACY'S POV from cab.

CHRIS and a SOLICITOR leave the station.

CHRIS

    Thanks a lot, mate.

They shake hands.

TRACY looks across to CHRIS.

CHRIS still looks shaken, surprised at the sudden release. He holds his stomach, he has been roughed up.

TRACY

You've been nothin' but trouble Chris. You screw up at Metro and then you have the nerve to drag me down here.

CHRIS

Bastards!... What was I supposed to tell 'em?... Oh, I was pirate broadcasting at the time, and my best mate hangs about in parks after dark...

TRACY

Chris, are you listening to me?

CHRIS

Tracy, I'm sorry. Thanks for gettin' the solicitor for us. Listen, I've got this tape, right? It was in the beat box.

TRACY

You've got to give it in, Chris.

CHRIS

What? Go back in there? You're jokin'.

TRACY

Look, I'm no friend of the police, but if it's evidence you're dealing with, you don't mess with it.

CHRIS

So I just let 'em drag my sister in for friendly questionin'?

TRACY

Yeah, yeah. Alright. Forget it. It's none of my business. Just keep me out of it... I've got to get back to work.

CHRIS looks disconsolate and confused.

TRACY

You look pathetic... Come on... I'll drop you off.

CHRIS climbs into the cab, TRACY pulls the door shut.

50 INT. GARAGE – Late afternoon

CHRIS plays the Park tape.

The crackly but just audible opening exchange:

VOICES ON TAPE:

WHITE MAN

Cute, aren't yer?

YOUNG BLACK MAN

So ya wanna get to know me?

WHITE MAN

Wot's yer name?

KEN arrives at the garage.

YOUNG BLACK MAN

Name? You a policeman or what?

WHITE MAN

Just being friendly, tell us yer name.

KEN crawls through the broken down car that blocks the back of the garage, the pirate base, to where CHRIS is listening to the tape.

YOUNG BLACK MAN (on tape)

Man, you're one stubborn white boy.

CHRIS is startled by KEN.

KEN

Chris... Brought you something... it's out the front... Give us a hand, it's a bit 'eavy...

YOUNG BLACK MAN (on tape)

Terry, friends call me T.J.

CHRIS turns off the tape, ejects and pockets it.

CHRIS

Be right wiv yer, Mr Stylee!

51 EXT. TOWERBLOCK/ROOFTOP – Dusk

CHRIS and CAZ carry a new aerial onto the roof, CHRIS at the front, CAZ at the back. They negotiate an awkward hatch that leads up on to the roof. They're sweating. On the roof - they clap hands in air. They rest on a ledge.

CAZ

Twice as many soul patrollers! Neva enough for you though, is it? Won't rest till you're on Radio One!

CHRIS (In BBC accent)

This is the BBC Soul Service. Are you sitting comfortably?

They set to work, laughing at the thought. But CHRIS is still distracted, tense after the police questioning. Thinking back.

CHRIS

What really fucks me in all this is they were questionin' ma sista! A nine-year old girl! Is like they're goin' wild. Ye know wot I mean?

CAZ

Pure slackness, man!

CHRIS steps towards a pole, holds the new aerial against the pole. It's right at the edge of the rooftop. CAZ stands by with a roll of heavy-duty sticking tape.

CAZ

I'll keep dog.

CHRIS

Kelly was in there. I mean, what is it? 'Let's Get The Half-Caste Week' or something?

CHRIS is still shaky from the interrogation. Dangerously close to the edge. Suddenly CHRIS slips, hangs over the side of the tower block. He screams out.

Tilt down: the dizzying height of the block, the ground far below.

CHRIS clings to the aerial, CAZ grabs him, carefully pulls him back to safety.

CAZ

You were nearly a gonna, man! Right, no more time up 'ere, let's just do the ting and get down.

CHRIS

Thanks, man.

They move back from the edge. Finally satisfied with their handiwork, and relieved it's done, they embrace. They cross the roof to go back down.

CHRIS

Oh... yeah... Tracy fixed up a meeting with this producer down Metro. It was her that got me out of the nick.

CAZ

Are you serious? You been crawlin' round Metro again?

CHRIS

Caz, I've got to get some steady....

CAZ (mimics Chris)

'Some steady money in'. *I* got us the fuckin' aerial, right? You think I like doing Ken favours? Draggin' me bruvver into it? Carlton's gonna let a car go cheap for me and you, ya know...

CHRIS

Metro weren't interested, so just forget it, right?

CAZ

Chris, I'm just sayin'. We *are* gettin through - there's an audience buildin'. We'll get the advertisin' and we'll 'ave the money...

CHRIS

Look, you was tryin' your way, I was tryin' mine. It's the same thing.

CAZ

I wanted a partner, not your fuckin' vanity!

CHRIS suddenly puts his arm round CAZ.

CHRIS

Caz, I am your partner, Caz. We gonna hit the airwaves, yeah? Funk the Jubilee special!

CAZ

I can't tomorrow. Said I'd play the concert tomorrow wiv that punk I met – Billibudd.

CHRIS

Don't joke about it, Caz.

CAZ

I promised.

CHRIS jumps back up to the aerial.

CHRIS

Might as well smash it down then, mightn't I? 'Cos Caz can't be bovvered. He'd sooner go off wiv some BILLEE-BUDD to play for a bunch of middle class punks an' hippies – wankers Caz. Where's your loyalty man? Where's the fuckin' loyalty in that?

CAZ

Where's the loyalty in you going behin' ma back, struttin' roun' Metro, prattlin' bout what we're doin'? Ain't you got no sense? A quick word wiv the Home Office and they can 'ave a station like ours wiped out before breakfast... I thought I was supposed to be your main man?

CHRIS

What are you talkin' about? You are ma main man. I've 'ad a day of it, right? An' a bit of sympathy might be in order...

CAZ

Cry on Tracy's shoulder...

CHRIS

I'm gonna smash that thing...

CHRIS turns to the aerial...

CAZ

Smash it, you might as well.

CAZ leaves the roof. CHRIS calls after him.

CHRIS

Caz, I ain't begun to tell yer 'bout what 'appened down the nick.

CAZ

I ain't got the time, I'm gonna and go an' see Billi.

CAZ leaves the roof, furious. He doesn't hear Chris's words, or see the Park tape that CHRIS takes out from his pocket...

CHRIS

Caz... See this tape, Caz? It's TJ's tape...

52 EXT. WEST-END STREETS – Night

CAZ and BILLIBUDD are out for the night. BILLIBUDD's daytime politico wear is replaced by a sexier, night-time punk style. He's also wearing black eye make-up.

CAZ and BILLI steer a course through a pedestrianised part of central London. There are book and ballet shops, jewellers and smart hairdressers. Attempts at upmarket Jubilee displays in many of the windows.

CAZ and drink from cans of imported lager. They're laughing, exhilarated.

BILLIBUDD has something to say to half the passers-by, his first victim is a WOMAN in evening dress.

BILLIBUDD

Bomb the rich! Bomb the rich!

BAY CITY ROLLERS fans in full fan regalia roll by.

BILLIBUDD

Bay City Rollers, why don't yer listen to some decent music, eh?

CAZ remains a bit detached, part enjoying BILLI's outgoing cheek, part unsure.

There's a bookshop with racks of books on sale outside. 'Gay News' on sale inside. Mary Whitehouse and Anita Bryant making the headlines. The shop stocks a mix of respectable gay novels – Gide, Cocteau, Genet – and old muscle magazines, like 'Adonis' and 'Body Beautiful'. Collector gay porn.

Posters for Divine and Nureyev, both on in town.

A MAN BROWSING.

BILLIBUDD grabs a book, collars the man.

BILLIBUDD
    Jean Genet, ever read that, 'ave yer? Eh? Eh?

BILLI disturbs the book rack, flicks at postcards on revolving stands. The MAN mutters politely, embarrassed, a bit afraid.

MAN
    Thank you... yes .. yes... I have.

A MAN with a DOG passes by.

BILLIBUDD
    Look after your bloody dog....

BILLI picks up a book and throws it for CAZ to catch. A WINDOW-DRESSER stares out from a tasteful array of ballet frocks. He stares at BILLI, BILLI stares back.

BILLIBUDD
    What you looking at? Piss off...

BILLI and CAZ watch the WINDOW-DRESSER complete the display. He looks distinctly nervous.

It's not only BILLI and CAZ who are watching. THREE SCOTLAND SUPPORTERS reel in. They're in town for the England/Scotland match. One of them is shirtless and kilted. A flag draped over his shoulders.

BILLI watches the shirtless man. The shirtless Scot sings and chants:
    Scotland, Scotland'...

BILLIBUDD raises his arm, clenches his fist. Shows solidarity with the Scottish cause.

BILLIBUDD
    Devloution now!

The shirtless SUPPORTER steps up to BILLIBUDD.

SUPPORTER
    Fuck off, ye Southern poofter!

BILLIBUDD lowers his arm...

TWO WOMEN pass the shirtless SUPPORTER.

SUPPORTER
    Gie us a kiss, darlin'!

WOMAN
Fuck off!

The other two SUPPORTERS sing and chant anti-English songs, laugh at the posh shop displays.

A mad, chaotic clash of people and styles, everyone out on the town, enjoying the hot, summer night.

53 EXT. GAY CLUB ENTRANCE – Night

BILLIBUDD and CAZ arrive at the entrance to a gay club. It is guarded by BOUNCERS.

CAZ and BILLI wait to be let in.

A BOUNCER blocks THREE BLACK SOUL BOYS who are trying to get in.

BOUNCER 1
Look boys. It's gay tonight. Official policy. No straights. Fuck off.
1st BLACK SOUL BOY
Leave it out. What you talkin' bout man? We're gay.
BOUNCER 1
No membership card. No entry. Simple. 'Op it.

TWO WHITE BOYS pass straight through, no membership cards shown.

2nd BLACK SOUL BOY
You let them in...
BOUNCER 2
I recognised their faces.
2nd BLACK SOUL BOY
Yeah. And we all look the same, right?

BILLIBUDD waves his card at the BLACK SOUL BOYS and the BOUNCERS.

BILLIBUDD
It's alright, alright. I've got a card, right... I'm allowed guests, huh?.
1st BLACK SOUL BOY
This club's got some crisp music, man. All we wanna do is check out the groove.

The BOUNCER decides in their favour, but glares at BILLI.

BOUNCER 1
Right. They're in. But if there's any trouble I'll personally ram that card down yer throat...

The BLACK SOULBOYS head into the disco.

The shirtless SCOTLAND SUPPORTER staggers down the road, sees the club. Calls his mates.

SCOTLAND SUPPORTER
'Ere boys, a club!

He looks up at the bulky BOUNCER.

SCOTLAND SUPPORTER

    Any chance of a dance, big fella?

BOUNCER 1

    Get out of it...

54 INT. CLUB CORRIDOR – Night.

Disco music reverberates in the corridor. Sylvester: 'You Make Me Feel (Mighty Real)'

CAZ and BILLIBUDD walk a little way into the club.

CAZ

    What would we do without ya, Blondie? Golden tongue, golden hair, golden boy!

BILLI looks baffled. CAZ ruffles his hair, mock-affectionate

A parade of clubgoers squeeze past them in the corridor. The mix of '77 gay style: Brixton radical drag and neo-hippie, US moustache macho, suburban 'wedge queen' (geometrically styled haircuts), rent boy and punk.

But for all the mix it is almost entirely male and almost entirely white.

A GAY GUY eyes Caz up, as he walks past he strokes CAZ's arm, brushes against him. The gay guy's FRIEND notices...

FRIEND

    Mary, you are *such* a dinge queen...

BILLIBUDD catches the comment and grabs the FRIEND's arm.

BILLIBUDD

    Oi you, fuck off....

CAZ takes BILLI's hand off the man. CAZ turns to leave the club. BILLIBUDD follows.

55 EXT. CLUB – Night

BILLI takes chewing gum from his mouth.

Leaned against the club wall, CAZ and BILLI kiss.

A passing STRAIGHT COUPLE look startled by the sight. The MAN mutters, 'disgusting'.

56 EXT. METRO RADIO/ROOFTOP – Night

A warm night. The roof lit by safety lamps and the moon. TRACY breathes in the air.

TRACY

    Makes me feel like a criminal, sneaking in here at night!

CHRIS

    We ain't doing no harm.

TRACY

We'll wait till the cleaners have gone from the studio.

CHRIS lays his jacket down on a skylight. He sits on his jacket. TRACY joins him. They looks over the city.

57 EXT. CAR – Night

CAZ and BILLI in the car. CAZ looks moody.

BILLIBUDD

You annoyed?

CAZ

Should've given him a good slap!

BILLI laughs.

CAZ

I've been thinkin'... about Soul Patrol... me and Chris, it ain't workin'. Told you about him getting nicked today, didn't I? Well I wasn't exactly sympathetic.

BILLIBUDD

Caz, you talk about him a lot. I mean... what... You two do it, then?

CAZ

Why? What's it to you?

BILLIBUDD

Nothing Caz, no. I just want to know, that's all. You do realise I fancy you, don't you?... Fancy you a lot.

CAZ quietly smiles.

CAZ

Yeah, well, I did sleep with Chris for a coupla months. His Mum was in hospital at the time, having Trish, his little sister. Chris stayed over at my house...

BILLIBUDD looks a bit dejected.

BILLIBUDD

So he is gay then? I thought he was.

CAZ

Well.... we were about ten at the time! He turned out straight. Sad story really!

CAZ and BILLI both laugh.

BILLIBUDD

Caz, are you seeing anyone?

CAZ

I'm seeing you, ain't I?

The car passes underneath the bridge seen earlier. The NF sign has been spraycanned over with 'Black and White Unite and Fight'.

BILLIBUDD

Black and white unite and fuck!

BILLI laughs at his own joke. CAZ is only half amused. He raises his eyebrows, as if to ask, what *is* this man like?

58 EXT. METRO RADIO – Night

TRACY and CHRIS kiss.

TRACY unbuttons Chris's shirt.

She strokes his chest, pushes the shirt off his shoulders.

She runs her fingers across his crotch. Slowly she moves astride him, pulling back her long skirt. CHRIS quickly undoes his flies.

CHRIS moans and mutters as they make love.

TRACY is half touched by his words, half laughing. For a moment she breaks the rhythm.

TRACY
    Less of the patter, DJ...

Slow love-making, cries of pleasure.

Their shirts ripple in the wind.

DISSOLVE TO: later that night

59 INT. METRO RADIO STUDIO – Night

Myriad yellow, red and green lights. Almost darkness.

TRACY at the control desk. The Park cassette is in a machine. CHRIS and TRACY listen, TRACY adjusts controls for optimum sound.

VOICES ON TAPE:

YOUNG BLACK MAN
    So ya wanna get to know me?
WHITE MAN
    Wot's yer name?
YOUNG BLACK MAN
    Name? You a policeman or what?
WHITE MAN
    Just being friendly, tell us yer name.
YOUNG BLACK MAN
    Man, you're one stubborn white bwoy. OK – Terry. Friends call me T.J.

Sounds of struggle...

Close on the glowing red studio clock.

TRACY switches the machine off.

CHRIS
    Is that it?

TRACY

That's enough.

CHRIS

No... There's more...There's more...

TRACY

Game's over, Chris. It *is* weird, I don't like it.

CHRIS

Jus' lemme listen again.

TRACY

Look, if that's what that tape sounds like, you've got to hand it over.

CHRIS

Look... I just want to copy it...

TRACY

Okay...

They work fast to copy the tape.

VOICES FROM TAPE:

WHITE MAN

Like it down 'ere, do yer? Come down 'ere regular?

YOUNG BLACK MAN

Yeah...

Later: Close up: CHRIS packages a copy of the tape.

The address on the package:
TERRY JAMES CASE
DALSTON POLICE STATION
LONDON E8

CHRIS seals the flap.

TRACY watches. They kiss. CHRIS picks up his jacket.

They leave.

60 **EXT. STREETS NEAR ESTATE – Day**

CAZ and BILLIBUDD walk near the estate. BILLIBUDD stops as they near area the drive-way into the estate.

CAZ

So why are we stoppin'?

BILLIBUDD

Thought we'd drop in on the party.

BILLI reaches into his canvas bag full of leaflets and newspapers.

CAZ

Oh yeah, thinkin' of doin' a bit of canvassin' are we? Forget it...

BILLIBUDD

Course not, Caz. Course not. Just thought I'd tell a few more people about the concert, you know? Funk the Jubilee! Caz at the controls – right?

CAZ

Spare me, Billi...

BILLIBUDD

Don't worry 'bout it, I'll be a good boy. I won't be an embarrassment.

CAZ

Embarrass yaself as much as you like. Just leave me out of it.

A MAN in DRAG from the estate JUBILEE party glares at them. At evident gayness, at punk versions of the Queen (on BILLI's shirt), at black and white boy together. He forgets the incongruity of his own get-up.

CAZ follows BILLI into the estate.

INTERCUT WITH:

61 INT. GARAGE/RADIO – Day

CHRIS moves towards the radio base at the back of the garage. He calls for CAZ. There is no reply.

With a shock he sees a mesh of brown tape curled up round his feet. There is brown tape everywhere. Their every cassette has been unwound and ruined. Roughly spelt out in cut-up tape – an NF sign.

Shards of broken cassette boxes crack under CHRIS's feet. Yet the records and the equipment are left intact.

CHRIS is totally unnerved.

Nevertheless he climbs through the wrecked car entry to the pirate base.

He switches the turntable. He carefully selects a record, steadying himself. Puts on headphones.

He picks up the mike, begins to play Funkadelic: 'One Nation Under A Groove'.

His voice is fragmented, shocked.

CHRIS

'One Nation Under A Groove'... and most of all right now... we're going out to my main man, Caz... Funk the Jubilee... Hold tight... The groove's travellin' on the park tonight... Main man Caz is gonna be... funkin' the Jubilee...An' if you ain't gonna be there... you ain't gonna be nowhere... I'll see you later Caz... nuff luv...

The song goes on:

... this is a chance/this is a chance/to dance your way/out of your constrictions/... With the groove/our only guide/we shall all be moved... One nation under a groove/gettin' down just for the funk of it/One nation and we're on the move/ Nothin' can stop us now...

CHRIS cries.

INTERCUT WITH:

62 EXT. ESTATE JUBILEE PARTY – Day

CAZ and BILLIBUDD at the street party, enclosed in the estate courtyard.

The estate has been transformed into a riot of red, white and blue. Flags everywhere. Tables decked out for a meal, stalls selling all manner of Jubilee junk.

Children take turns to sit inside a huge gold-sprayed carriage made of cardboard and crates. They sit in serious mimicry of royals.

A YOUNG BLACK BOY cuts through the crowd on his chopper bike, riding directly at the carriage. Handlebars fill the screen. He looks set to crash but skids and steers sharply to avoid it. On the back of the bike - a Union Jack, blowing in the wind.

Many of the party-goers are in fancy dress, from BEEFEATERS to ELVIS PRESLEY.

BILLI relishes the sight, can't wait to send it up. He heads for a stall and grabs a Jubilee fan.

BILLIBUDD

This is nice. How much is this? Just the right thing for my 'friend'.

STALLKEEPER

Get yer bleedin' 'ands off...

BILLIBUDD heads down past a row of stalls, finally pausing at a goldfish stall. Ball in the bowl and you win a goldfish.

The GOLDFISH STALL MAN struggles to keep control as BILLI pokes at the fish prizes in their polythene bags.

BILLIBUDD

This is cruelty to animals. How'd you like to be stuffed up in a plastic bag? This your idea of fun, is it? You're sick, you are.

BILLI turns his attention to a MIDDLE-AGED COUPLE, he proffers a copy of *Socialist Worker.*

BILLIBUDD

Oi... *Socialist Worker,* right? Stuff the Jubilee .. the only paper for the working class... look, we're having a party down the park, why don't yer come down, have a look?

The MAN pushes BILLI away.

MAN

Just piss off...

A GIRL notices the row...

GIRL

Wot was that all about, then?

She stares at BILLI.

INTERCUT WITH

63 **INT. GARAGE/RADIO – DAY (continued)**

CHRIS on his own.

End of 'Running Away' on the tape...

KEN appears in the background, remarks on the mess.

KEN

Hi... blimey... what 'appened?

CHRIS

Not now Ken, I'm in the middle of a show, mate.

KEN

D'yer call the police?

CHRIS shakes his head, 'No'.

CHRIS

Nah, it's no use... no use...

KEN calmly closes in on CHRIS.

Suddenly KEN smashes out, pushing CHRIS over the desk...

CHRIS

What yer doin'... ?

KEN knocks the tape deck to the floor.

KEN

You know wot I want. You fuck me about and I'll kill yer.

KEN has CHRIS by the throat, he tightens his grip.

KEN

Always thought you were so smart, didn't yer? Well I set you up... I set you up
nicely...

CHRIS struggles... KEN's speech is disjointed, a struggle to force the words out...

KEN

Since when've you fuckin' cared? You don't understand... you're not like Caz...
Thought I'd kill two birds with one stone.... But pretty boy...

KEN pulls CHRIS round to face him. He grips CHRIS's face.

KEN

You pretty boy... You had to stick yer nose in. Gimme the tape, Chris... give me the
fucking tape!

CHRIS

I 'aven't got it...

CHRIS summons all his force to push KEN off. They fall to the ground fighting.

CHRIS kicks out. Kicks KEN in the face...

CHRIS dives through the car at the back of the garage... runs towards the street...

KEN has lost him.

KEN wipes his bloodied face...

INTERCUT WITH:

64 EXT. ESTATE JUBILEE PARTY – Day (continued)

ANN, CHRIS's mother, walks through the estate. She's cornered by an elderly BLUE-RINSED WHITE WOMAN.

BLUE RINSE
> Lovely atmosphere, innit Ann? Remember what it used to be like round 'ere? When you could leave your door open an' not worry 'bout bleeding muggers - or worse...

ANN
> Yeah. I reckon I know what you mean Lil, reckon I know.

A YOUNGER WOMAN passes by. She greets BLUE RINSE. She carries a copy of a National Front newspaper.

WOMAN
> *National Front News...*

ANN grabs the paper from the startled YOUNGER WOMAN. She glances across the headlines:'Hundreds of Thousands Turn Out to Vote National Front!'

ANN slowly tears the newspaper apart, scatters it on the ground.

The YOUNG WOMAN backs off, angry but a bit afraid of ANN.

TRISH and her FRIENDS are nearby.

FRIEND
> Trish, there's your Mum...

TRISH
> Mum!

TRISH runs up to ANN. ANN kisses her on the forehead.

ANN
> Alright, babes? You enjoyin' yerself?

TRISH
> Yeah...

TRISH is clutching a small radio. There's a small Union Jack sticking out of the machine. ANN takes the radio and snaps off the flag.

ANN
> Here, come on, yer don't need that.

She hands the flag-free radio back.

ANN
> Let's go over the park, eh? And get some clean air.

CAZ approaches.

CAZ

'Lo Ann. You ain't seen some punk walkin' about, 'ave ya?

ANN

Not noticed. Wot are you doin 'ere anyways?

CAZ

Passin' through fast. You goin' over the Park?

ANN

Yeah, thought we might go for an hour. Then I thought I might drop round your Mum's.

TRISH tugs at CAZ's waistcoat.

TRISH

Did you 'ear Chris on the radio?

CAZ

What? Been on air, 'as he?

TRISH

Said about the Park, said you'd be on, Mr 'Main Man'.

CAZ

He talked about the park?

ANN

Why ain't yer workin' wiv 'im today, Caz? You alright, you and Chris?

TRISH interrupts.

TRISH

Soul Patrol went dead!

CAZ

That bloody equipment...!

CAZ continues to look for BILLI.

ANN

Catch yer later, babes.

CAZ

Right...

TRISH

Bye...

CUT TO: BILLIBUDD at a stall run by a PEARLY KING and QUEEN.

BILLIBUDD

So what's all this then?

PEARLY KING

It's a raffle, and you 'ave to 'ave a ticket.

BILLIBUDD

A raffle. Alright, give us a ticket, then.

The PEARLY QUEEN opens a book of tickets. BILLI mauls the prizes.

BILLIBUDD

After Eights, huh?

BILLI puts down the chocolates and snatches the whole book of tickets.

BILLIBUDD
'S alright, darling, don't worry, I'll take the lot.
PEARLY KING
Oi, oi - where's yer money?
BILLIBUDD
Whoa .. whoa... alright, hold on...

The PEARLY QUEEN grabs the book of tickets back.

BILLIBUDD reahces into his bag and pulls out a newspaper. Starts his sales patter again.

BILLIBUDD
Have one of these, *Socialist Worker* .. Only paper for the working class... look - free membership on the back... don't worry about it ..
PEARLY KING
Oi you, fuck off out of it and take that shit wiv yer!
BILLIBUDD
Wait, wait, wait... So what's your problem, eh? What's your problem?

Looking across at BILLIBUDD: perched on the rubbish sheds: the skins, KELLY, BIGGSY, SPARKY...

BILLI continues to aggravate the PEARLY KING.

BILLIBUDD
Why don't you read this sometime? It might educate yer.
PEARLY KING
Go on .. on your way...

Suddenly a beercan is hurled from the sheds, it catches BILLIBUDD across the face. It cuts him just above the eye.

As BILLI holds his face a conga of Jubilee revellers curls past him.

The beercan carrying SKINS jump down to close in on BILLI.

CAZ arrives.

SPARKY
Better get yer noo boyfriend 'art of 'ere 'ere Caz, or else 'e might need carryin'...

BILLI is panicked. CAZ more casual about it. He can usually handle SPARKY and Co. He pushes SPARKY and BIGGSY aside, leads BILLI through the skins.

CAZ ignores the taunts, the crushing of cans, the gestures...

Safely away, CAZ rounds on BILLI. But at the same time as he shouts he wipes the blood from BILLI'S face, tends him. Some of the blood has dripped down onto the t-shirt image of the Queen.

CAZ
You stupid fuckin' wanker. You can't listen to no-one, can ya?

BILLIBUDD

I was only doing my paper round, Caz!

CAZ

You're well out of order, Blondie. You're always shoutin' 'bout imperialism... jus' look at yaself...

BILLIBUDD looks bemused.

CAZ

You think if it's there, yer can take it, dont ya? Ya think you can go where the fuck ya like.

BILLIBUDD

But I'm wiv you Caz.

CAZ

Yeah, well that depends... dunnit?

BILLIBUDD

We're still playing the park, aren't we?

CAZ

Plenty of time for that. Let's get your face fixed, Blondie.

CAZ wipes blood from BILLI's face.

BILLIBUDD

Why'd you keep calling me Blondie? I'm not even blond.

CAZ

Don't worry about it. You're near enough.

They embrace, head away from the estate.

65 INT. BILLIBUDD'S FLAT – Day

More flags on a wall, but these are inside, they're ripped and defaced or plastered in punk imagery...

Billi's room is as much a shrine to Punk as the garage is to Reggae - skip furnished, vinyl chairs and dead branches of a tree forming a bed board of sorts.

BILLI comes into the room, an icepack over the cut on his face, a beer bottle at his mouth. CAZ takes a cigarette. BILLI puts on X-Ray Spex: 'Identity'.

Climbs on the bed, takes off his studded belt.

CAZ laughs at the choice of music, turns the record off.

BILLI

Not the best idea... Agreed!

BILLI climbs off the bed. Kisses CAZ then sorts through his mostly punk records, finally he finds a reggae song. Junior Murvin: 'Police and Thieves'.

Another kiss. CAZ laughs at the attempt to seduce with black music, the record goes the same way as the first.

CAZ
    'Ow about quiet?

They walk towards the bed. CAZ takes off BILLI's shirt, kisses the plaster on his face. Places his cigarette into BILLI's mouth.

BILLI takes off CAZ's shirt. They move to the bed. BILLI kisses CAZ's chest... and moves down his body.

Gulps of beer, drags at the cigarette, undressing...

Then the slow thump of serious pleasure.

66 EXT. ESTATE – late afternoon.

The debris of the Jubilee party. A messy, bleak, near deserted courtyard.

A voice-over from a the Queen's broadcast.

QUEEN (VOICE-OVER)
    At the Silver Jubilee of 1935... and at my Coronation...

Flags flutter in the wind.

The wind's dry metallic sound.

CHRIS runs into the estate.

Just a few JUBILEE STRAGGLERS are left, a couple heading drunkenly home, a couple clearing the mess from their doorsteps.

CHRIS kicks a can along the ground.

QUEEN (VOICE-OVER CNTD.)
    ... the Empire and the Commonwealth came to London...

CHRIS collides with an abandoned pram... it rolls across the courtyard.
KEN's voice still in his head.

KEN (VOICE-OVER)
    Give me the tape Chris. Give me the fucking tape.

QUEEN (VOICE-OVER)
    ... the travelling is in both directions...and I think we can claim to be doing our fair share...

CHRIS looks round the estate, searching. Finally he runs out.

67 EXT. PARK – Late afternoon

Distant sounds of music in the Park.

TRACY and JILL from arrive for the concert, JILL is now dressed soul-girl style, a total convert. They run into CAZ and BILLIBUDD.

TRACY

Caz... You're Caz, aren't you? Chris's other half, er, DJ spa, right? We never did get properly introduced at the Club. Where is he? Have you seen him?

CAZ

Yeah, he's my other half. An' you're Tracy from Metro... I hear they're letting us in now, one at a time. That's really metropolitan of 'em...

TRACY

What are you talking about? I don't 'ave to justify what I do to you.

TRACY takes in BILLI's 'clean' t-shirt. It features two cowboys, naked from the waist down....

CAZ

Chris was on the air this afternoon. It seems he got cut off. Metro had any pirates taken off the air lately, has it?

TRACY

Come on!

BILLIBUDD

Capitalist crap, Metro Radio.

CAZ

Shut up, Billi.

TRACY

Spending twenty pounds on T-shirts from Vivienne Westwood has got nothing to do with capitalism, hmmm?

BILLIBUDD

It has to do with homoerotica. Nicked homoerotica, actually. Like it?

TRACY

Luv it. It's like Anarchy courtesy of EMI... so rebellious... so St Martin's School of Art... excuse me.

CAZ has to smile at the send-up of BILLI.

TRACY leaves.

TRACY

Come on, Jill...

JILL

Coming...

CAZ taps BILLI in the stomach, time to move on...

CUT TO:

68 EXT. ESTATE – early evening.

CHRIS returns to the estate, still searching. Bunting dropped from a balcony falls across his path.

A voice calls out to him.

VOICE

Oi, soulboy!

CHRIS looks up to see SPARKY, KELLY and BIGGS.

Closing in on him.

CHRIS walks straight up to KELLY.

CHRIS
Wot was they askin' yer down the nick?
KELLY
Wanted an 'alf caste. Told 'em they musta got the wrong one.
SPARKY
Oh dear, I forgot to wear me white suit.

CHRIS looks him up and down: the shaved head, Union Jack t-shirt, the patriotic skin-style.

CHRIS
You look pretty white to me.

The gang laugh.

SPARKY
Shut up! Don't know why *you're* laughin', Kelly.

KELLY stops laughing.

CHRIS
Kelly laughs at anythin', 'cos he knows nothin'. And as long as he knows nothin', he can make out he's whi...

KELLY shouts to drown the word 'white'.

KELLY
Wot's it to you?
CHRIS
Ain't nothing to me, it's only yerself yer connin'.

SPARKY smiles, enjoys CHRIS and KELLY arguing it out amongst themselves. CHRIS knows SPARKY would relish a fight.

Instead CHRIS walks up to KELLY, he grabs him, pulls him close.
CHRIS is too angry to be worried by any of them.

CHRIS
Why're you lying and hidin' all the time, Kelly? They were pissing about wiv us down at the station. Ken killed T.J. and tried to pin it on us. You listenin'? Have you seen Ken?
KELLY
I ain't seen him, Chris. Honest.

CHRIS lets go of KELLY, KELLY stumbles backwards.

SPARKY crashes a milk bottle to the ground, it smashes close to CHRIS.

CHRIS starts to scream out.

CHRIS
> Caz. Where *are* you Caz?... Where are you?...Where are you?

The SKINS are confused and angered by Chris's behaviour, there's none of the usual banter. Neighbours come out of their doors, look down from their balconies. So many eyes on them, the gang can't risk a fight.

CHRIS keeps calling for Caz.

Even SPARKY is unnerved.

69 EXT. PARK – Night

CHRIS runs into the Park.

He pushes through punks and hippy-types.

Still shouting.

CHRIS
> Where are you?

There are heaps of banners and placards round the edge of the Park. Emblems of the Socialist Workers' Party, labour groups and trades' councils, mixed with the punkier graphics of the Anti-Nazi League. A sharp contrast to the Estate Jubilee decorations. CHRIS stumbles through the placards.

In the distance, a stage. A 'Fuck The Jubilee' banner emblazoned across it.

A short way from the main crowd, CHRIS spots TRACY and JILL. JILL is dancing with TWO BLACK WOMEN. Live music from an Asian band fills the Park.

TRACY catches sight of CHRIS.

TRACY
> There's Chris... Chris!...

CHRIS calls out to TRACY, TRACY leaves the WOMEN to reach him.

A blur of extraordinary images, seen selectively, in fragments, through Chris's anxious eyes. The 'Fuck the Jubilee' is as much a pageant as the Jubilee itself. People are decked out in masks, in parodies of Jubilee costumes. CHRIS pushes past the ASIAN GIRL PUNK, seen earlier with Billibudd leafleting the tube. She is dressed as Britannia, with spear and shield – an outfit to offend just about everybody.

The ASIAN PUNK GIRL's friends wear satiric and grotesque masks - of Callaghan, Steel...

Others wear clothes featuring distorted images of the Royal Family. A small group wear cardboard corgi masks.

Finally TRACY reaches CHRIS.

TRACY
> Chris!

CHRIS grabs hold of her arms. A panic in him.

CHRIS

　　Ken did it... it was Ken... Listen... something's gonna happen, I've gotta find Caz...

TRACY

　　Ssshhh... Slow down, Chris. Slow down. What are you talking about, who's Ken?

CHRIS

　　Just help me find him...

TRACY

　　No Chris. No more. We're going. Have you seen all the police? Vans loads of 'em, all round the park. I don't like the look of it...

CHRIS

　　Tracy... *please*...

CHRIS grabs TRACY, she sees all the fear in him and follows. They head for the stage...

CUT TO:

The stage. An Asian band pack away their instruments, unaware of the growing chaos round the edges of the park. They move to leave the stage for CAZ and BILLIBUDD to keep the disco going between acts. The stage is stacked with large, heavy speakers. Drum kits and electrical equipment.

CAZ steps up to the turntable, puts on a record.

CUT TO:

SPARKY and BIGGSY converge round the edge of the Park. They mix with a group of older men - many of them seen earlier in fancy-dress on the estate. A BEEFEATER, A POLICEMAN amongst them. Whether the policeman is real or not it's impossible to tell. The costumes make convenient masks. The men hand round bulging plastic bags.

CUT TO:

CHRIS and TRACY in the crowd. SKINS steam into the crowd... kicking people to the ground... CHRIS gets pushed... he loses TRACY.

CHRIS

　　Get off!... Tracy!... Tracy!

The surrounding fights get more vicious.

People, especially people with young children, are beginning to panic...

Gangs of NF thugs pick out the armbands of the Anti-Nazi League stewards, and move in to attack any who are on their own. Some of the Anti-Jubilee revellers run to the stewards' assistance.

The CID MAN from the police station is in the crowd, watching, not moving to anyone's assistance.

A man wearing a BEEFEATER costume lights a petrol bomb.

CAZ and BILLIBUDD survey the growing chaos from the stage.

A petrol bomb, seen close, pulled from a carrier bag... it hurtles through the air... a streak of light against a darkening sky.

The bomb hits the stage... starting a fire.

BILLI jumps down, CAZ tries to save the records, but in the middle of increasing chaos, some of the records spill onto the mud.

Roll over the ground.

CAZ
    Shit... Billi... the records ..

They have to make a run for it.

The stage banner is in flames.

Floodlights crash down on the crowd ..

CUT TO:

KEN runs into the Park. Pushes through the crowd. People are running to get out.

ANN tries to reach the Park gates with TRISH.

KEN bangs into ANN and TRISH, he knocks TRISH to the ground.

ANN yells after him as she picks TRISH up.

ANN
    Watch out... Are you all right?

She kisses TRISH, protects her as they move to get out.

They're surrounded by PUNKS and TEDS, PUNKS in anti-Nazi t-shirts, others in confusing swastikas...

CUT TO:

YEOMEN of the GUARD, BEEFEATERS, HENRY VIII, SIR WALTER RALEIGH, a group of heavily disguised men who work their way systematically towards the stage.

Screams and chaos.

Some of the Anti-Jubilee crowd tear at the flags and costumes of the Jubilee revellers. Carnival attacks Carnival. The police wade into selective Anti-Jubilee targets.

CUT TO:

CHRIS nears the stage. KEN in pursuit.

Smoke billows up, CHRIS can't see whether CAZ is still there.

SPARKY and BIGGS fall about laughing at the destruction.

CUT TO:

CHRIS reaches the stage, only to find CAZ gone. He climbs through flame.

Storyboard of the riot scene by John Hewitt

63.6 cont -

63.7

63.8

63.9

63.10

63.11

63.12

63.12.

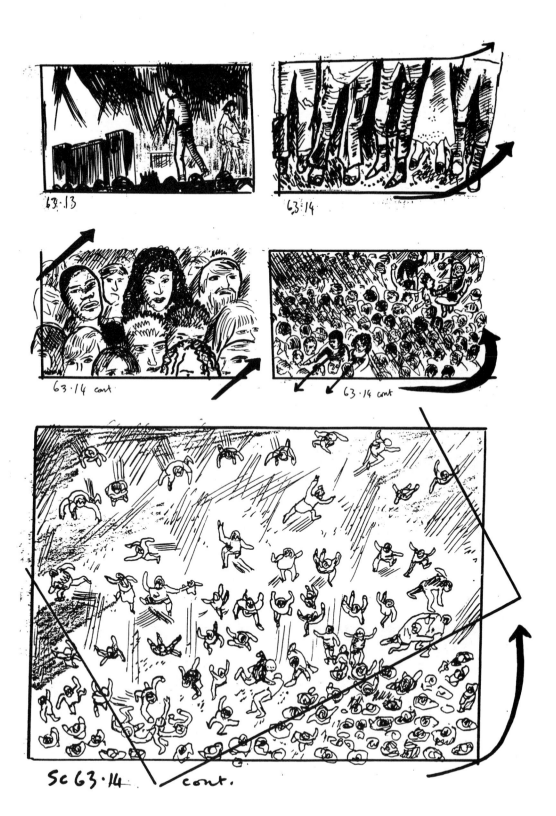

63·13

63·14

63·14 cont

63·14 cont

Sc 63·14   cont.

63.15

63.16

63.17

63.17 .

63.18

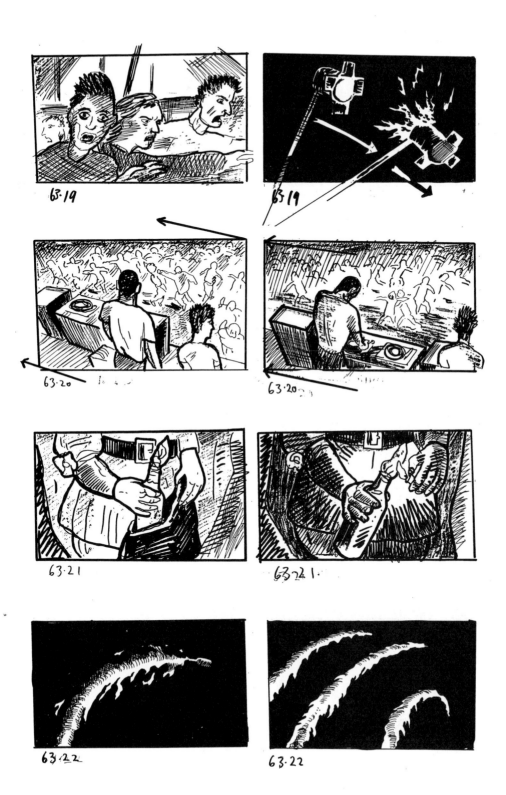

63·19

63·19

63·20

63·20

63·21

63·21

63·22

63·22

63·23

63·24

63·25

63·26

63·27

63·27

63·32

63·33

63· 34

63·35

63·35 cont

63·35 (A)

63·35 (B)

63·35 (C)

63·35 (D)

63·35 (E)

Takes the Park cassette out of his back pocket. Screams into the microphone.

The chill sound of KEN and T.J. in the opening scene, now broadcast across the Park.

CHRIS
I know you're here. Hear it!

VOICES ON TAPE:

T.J.
So leggo ma han'... I ain't into no rough stuff, right?
KEN
Cute, aren't yer?

CAZ and BILLIBUDD hear the tape... CAZ suddenly recognises the first voice.

CAZ
It's T.J.

VOICES ON TAPE (cntd)

T.J.
So ya wanna get to know me?

KEN
What's yer name?
T.J.
Name? You a policeman or what?

CAZ recognises the other voice.

CAZ
Ken!
KEN reaches the stage. Pushes and crawls through burning speakers to get to the tape deck. To stop the tape.

VOICES ON TAPE (cntd):

KEN
Just being friendly, tell us yer name.
T.J.
Man, you're one stubborn white bwoy.

CHRIS raises his arms to shield his face from the flames. He sees KEN coming towards him.

KEN tries to protect himself with his jacket hood. Suddenly part of the stage gives way under him. He disappears in flame.

CHRIS manages to jump off the stage just before the whole structure goes up in flame.

Screams from the crowd....

CUT TO:

Away from the stage area, the Park is emptying, quietening.

JILL cries. TRACY holds her, steadies her.

But there's also rage on TRACY'S face. Rage at the destruction.

CHRIS finds them...

CHRIS
> Tracy...

Not far away from CHRIS and TRACY, CAZ has covered his ears in horror. BILLIBUDD touches CAZ's face. BILLI tries to comfort him.

BILLIBUDD
> It's alright...

CAZ and CHRIS finally see each other...

CAZ
> Chris... Chris...

CHRIS leaves TRACY.
CHRIS
> Don't go. I'll be back.

CHRIS and CAZ step towards each other.

CHRIS
> Caz, thank Christ...

BILLIBUDD watches the meeting of CAZ and CHRIS

70 EXT. CITY – Night

Across rooftops. Night sky.

The garage.

71 INT. GARAGE – Same night. Towards dawn.

JILL and BILLIBUDD gently clean the mud off records rescued from the Park.

They've set up a kind of record repair production line. TRACY takes the polished records, passes them onto CHRIS and CAZ at the turntable.

CAZ and CHRIS test the records for playability, for scratches.

CHRIS turns to CAZ.

CHRIS
> I wasn't runnin' from yer, Caz. We're okay now, yeah? Soul Patrol again...
CAZ
> Yeah, let's start over...

They shake hands, then hold each other in a warm embrace.

CAZ
    Come on...

The records continue to pass from hand to hand... JILL steps out of the line to dance... TRACY joins JILL in the dance.

BILLIBUDD leaves the records to dance with TRACY and JILL.

CAZ moves from the turntable to join the dance...

CHRIS joins them...

Charles Earland: 'Let The Music Play.'

The laughter and the dance continue over:

                              END

FILMED ON LOCATION IN LONDON

A

THE BRITISH FILM INSTITUTE

FOR

FILM FOUR INTERNATIONAL

IN ASSOCIATION WITH

SANKOFA FILM & VIDEO,
LA SEPT, KINOWELT & IBEROAMERICANA

The events and persons, companies and institutions and other bodies portrayed in this film are wholly fictional and any resemblance to any real life situation or persons or entities whether existing now or in the past is purely coincidental.

© BFI MCMXCI

In memory of Mark Banks and Lucy Morahan

CAST

CHRIS	**Valentine Nonyela**
CAZ	**Mo Sesay**
KEN	**Dorian Healy**
ANN	**Frances Barber**
TRACY	**Sophie Okonedo**
BILLIBUD	**Jason Durr**
DAVIS	**Gary McDonald**
JILL	**Debra Gillett**
CARLTON	**Eamon Walker**
SPARKY	**James Bowyers**
KELLY	**Billy Braham**
BIGSY	**Wayne Norman**
TRISH	**Danielle Scillitoe**
JEFF KANE	**Ray Shell**
CID MAN	**Nigel Harrison**
PARK POLICEMAN	**John Wilson**
POLICEMAN NO. 1	**Brian Conway**
POLICEMAN NO. 2	**Mike Mungarvan**
ASIAN PUNK GIRL	**Sayan Akaddas**
TJ	**Shyro Chung**
BOUNCER	**Adam Price**
SOUL BOY NO. 1	**Michael Mascoll**
SOUL BOY NO.2	**Freddie Brooks**
IRVINE	**Rodriguez King-Dorset**
BARBER	**Lloyd Anderson**
MEN IN BARBER SHOP	**Adam Stuatt**
	Astley Harvey
RADIO PRODUCER	**Peter Harding**
FOOTBALL SUPPORTER	**Richard Jamieson**
STALLKEEPER	**Mark Brett**
BLUE RINSE LADY	**Joan Harsant**
TRISH'S FRIEND	**Verona Marshall**
TRISH'S FRIEND	**Frankie Palma**
STUNTMEN	**Stuart Clark**
	Antoni Garfield-Henry
	Nick Gillard
	Tim Lawrence
	Gareth Milne
	Mark Anthony Newman

CREW

CASTING	Gilly Poole and
	Suzanne Crowley
PRODUCTION MANAGER	Joanna Beresford
MUSIC SUPERVISORS	Bonnie Greenberg
	Ian P. Hierons
	Jill Meyers
EXECUTIVE IN CHARGE OF PRODUCTION	Angela Topping
COSTUME DESIGNER	Annie Curtis Jones
SOUND MIXER	Ronald Bailey
ORIGINAL MUSIC	Simon Boswell
PRODUCTION DESIGNER	Derek Brown
EDITOR	John Wilson
DIRECTOR OF PHOTOGRAPHY	Nina Kellgren
WRITERS	Paul Hallam
	Derrick Saldaan McClintock
	Isaac Julien
EXECUTIVE PRODUCERS	Colin MacCabe
	Ben Gibson
PRODUCED BY	Nadine Marsh-Edwards
DIRECTED BY	Isaac Julien
FIRST ASSISTANT DIRECTOR	Ian Ferguson
SECOND ASSISTANT DIRECTOR	Peter Heslop
SCRIPT SUPERVISOR	Angela Noakes
MAKE-UP ARTISTE	Yvonne Coppard
HAIR	Stephen Rose
LOCATION MANAGER	Michael Kelk
CONSTRUCTION MANAGER	Robin Thistlethwaite
PRODUCTION ACCOUNTANT	Angela Littlejohn
MUSICAL EFFECTS	Simon Fisher Turner
	Marvin Black
STUNT CO-ORDINATOR	Clive Curtis
PRODUCTION CO-ORDINATOR	Winnie Wishart
POST PRODUCTION CO-ORDINATOR	Eliza Mellor
CROWD CO-ORDINATOR	Jonny Kurzman
DIRECTORS ASSISTANTS	Rosemarie Hudson
	Michael McMillan
THIRD ASSISTANT DIRECTOR	Stephen Robinson
ACCOUNTS ASSISTANTS	Peter Smith
	Richard Beresford
	Sheryl Leonardo

UNIT RUNNERS	**Colin Fraser**
	Michelle McIntosh
	Orson Nava
JOBFIT PRODUCTION TRAINEE	**Gabrielle McNamara**
CAMERA OPERATOR/STEADICAM	**Andy Shuttleworth**
FOCUS PULLER	**Richard Philpott**
CLAPPER LOADER	**Ian Watts**
GRIP	**Mike House**
CAMERA TRAINEE	**Alessandra Scherillo**
CAMERA DRIVER	**Terry Mullins**
GAFFER	**Nuala Campbell**
ELECTRICIANS	**Simon Anderson**
	Ray Bateman
BOOM OPERATOR	**Martin Culverwell**
SOUND ASSISTANT	**Michelle Mascoll**
ART DIRECTOR	**Debra Overton**
ASSISTANT ART DIRECTORS	**Lucy Morahan**
	Michael Carter
STORYBOARD ARTIST	**John Hewitt**
PROPERTY BUYER	**Gina Cromwell**
PROPS MASTER	**Patrick Begley**
STANDBY PROPS	**Terry Tague**
ART DEPARTMENT ASSISTANT	**Linda Brown**
STANDBY CONSTRUCTION	**Tom Bowyer**
STANDBY RIGGER	**Clive Andrews**
CARPENTERS	**Geoff Stainthorpe**
	David Willams
SCENIC ARTISTS	**Joanna Craze**
	Annie Lapaz
CONSTRUCTION RUNNER	**Hugo Martin**
ART DEPARTMENT RUNNERS	**Joanna Tague**
	Stephan Lhoest
JOBFIT ART DEPARTMENT TRAINEE	**Martyn Wilson**
WARDROBE SUPERVISOR	**Caroline Pitcher**
WARDROBE MASTER	**Anthony Black**
WARDROBE MISTRESS	**Lisa M Johnson**
WARDROBE ASSISTANT	**Sheila Hailatt**
COSTUME ADVISERS	**Joey Attawia**
	Debbie Little
MAKE-UP/HAIR TRAINEE	**Tammy Harewood**
DUBBING EDITOR	**Zane Hayward**
DIALOGUE EDITOR	**Patrick O'Neill**
ADR EDITOR	**Shirley Shaw**

DUBBING MIXER	**Aad Wirtz**
FOLEY ARTIST	**Jack Stew**
FIRST ASSISTANT EDITOR	**Maxine Matts**
JOBFIT EDITING TRAINEES	**Fiona Walsh**
	Jo Crily
ADDITIONAL SOUND EFFECTS	**Steve Farrer**
	Nigel Heath
TECHNICAL SUPERVISOR	**Andy Powell**
SPECIAL FX SUPERVISOR	**Tom Harris**
CHOREOGRAPHY	**Foster George**
PUBLICITY	**Liz Reddish**
STILLS	**David A Bailey**
	Sunil Gupta
CONSTRUCTION	**London Film Construction**
SPECIAL EFFECTS	**Any Effects**
CATERERS	**Good Eating**
CAMERA EQUIPMENT	**Media Film Services**
ELECTRICAL EQUIPMENT	**GBS Film Lighting Ltd**
FILM LABORATORIES	**Metrocolor**
OPTICALS	**Studio 51**
TITLES	**Neville Brody**
	Frameline
RE-RECORDED AT	**Ladbroke Films (Dubbing) Ltd**
MUSIC CLEARANCE	**Media MusiConsultants**

2ND UNIT

DIRECTORS OF PHOTOGRAPHY	**Steve Tickner**
	Mike Metcalf
FOCUS PULLER	**Ian Watts**
SOUND	**Martine Couche**
CLAPPER LOADERS	**Mary Rose Noel**
	Roz Naylor
1ST ASSISTANT DIRECTORS	**Ian Hickinbotham**
	Bill Rudgard
2ND ASSISTANT DIRECTOR	**Jonny Kurzman**
3RD ASSISTANT DIRECTORS	**John Withers**
	Steve Millson
SCRIPT SUPERVISOR	**Susie Clegg**
CONSTRUCTION	**Stuart Wood**

WITH SPECIAL THANKS TO

John Akomfrah • Karen Alexander • Karin Bamborough • Paula Bernstock • Maureen Blackwood
Julian Cole • Stuart Cosgrove • E.A.V.E. • Elvis da Costa • Robert Crusz • Gregory Davis • Christine Duyt
Greg Edwards • Constantine Giannaris • Paul Gilroy • June Givanni • Renee Godard • David Harrison
Mick Hurd • Esther Johnson • Chris Kelly • Trevor Mathison • Drew Meldon • Mark Nash
Runnymead Trust • Jon Savage • Matthew Scott • Searchlight • Schoeps Microphones
Technics Panasonic • Anna Thew • John Tusa • Vron Ware • Pedro Williams

MUSIC CREDITS

"P. Funk Wants To Get Funked Up"
PERFORMED BY
Parliament
LICENSED COURTESY OF
Casablanca Record Inc/
Polygram Records Inc (New York)

"Rock Creek Park"
PERFORMED BY
The Blackbyrds
LICENSED COURTESY OF
Fantasy Inc

"I Like It"
PERFORMED BY
The Players Association
LICENSED COURTESY OF
Vangard, A Welk Music Group Company
BY ARRANGEMENT WITH
Warner Special Products

"Let's Get It Together"
PERFORMED BY
El Coco
LICENSED COURTESY OF
Philadelphia International Records Inc

"Say You Will"
PERFORMED BY
Eddie Henderson
LICENSED COURTESY OF
Capitol Records
BY ARRANGEMENT WITH
Cena Special Markets

"One Nation Under A Groove"
PERFORMED BY
Funkadelic
LICENSED COURTESY OF
Westbound Records Inc

"I'll Play The Fool"
PERFORMED BY
Dr. Buzzard
LICENSED COURTESY OF
BMG RCA Records Ltd

"You Make Me Feel (Mighty Real)"
PERFORMED BY
Sylvester
LICENSED COURTESY OF
Fantasy Inc

"Let The Music Play"
PERFORMED BY
Charles Earland
LICENSED COURTESY OF
Casablanca Records Inc/
Polygram Records Inc (New York)

"Identity"
PERFORMED BY
X-Ray Spex
LICENSED COURTESY OF
Awesome Records Ltd

"Running Away"
PERFORMED BY
Roy Ayers
LICENSED COURTESY OF
Casablanca Records Inc/
Polygram Records Inc (New York)

"Party Time"
PERFORMED BY
The Heptones
LICENSED COURTESY OF
Island Records Ltd

"Cocaine"
PERFORMED BY
Sly And The Revolutionaries
LICENSED COURTESY OF
Trojan Recordings Ltd

"Time Is Moving On"
PERFORMED BY
The Blackbyrds
LICENSED COURTESY OF
Fantasy Inc

"Oh Bondage Up Yours"
PERFORMED BY
X-Ray Spex
LICENSED COURTESY OF
EMI Records Ltd

"Me & My Baby Brother"
PERFORMED BY
War
LICENSED COURTESY OF
Avenue Records Inc

"Police & Thieves"
PERFORMED BY
Junior Murvin
LICENSED COURTESY OF
Island Records Ltd

"Message In Our Music"
PERFORMED BY
The O'Jays
LICENSED COURTESY OF
Philadelphia International Records

TITLE TRACK PERFORMED BY
The Chimes
LICENSED COURTESY OF
Columbia Records

Colin MacCabe and son, Finn, a notable extra in the Jubilee scene Photo by David Bailey

THE LIBRARY
TOWER HAMLETS COLLEGE
POPLAR HIGH STREET
LONDON E14 0AF
TEL: 071-538 5888